TIM GENT

# CAMPFIRE COOKING

Photographs by Tim and Susannah Gent

First published in 2017

Published in Great Britain 2017 by Pesda Press

Tan y Coed Canol

Ceunant

Caernarfon

Gwynedd

LL55 4RN

Copyright © 2017 Tim Gent

ISBN   9781906095611

The Author asserts the moral right to be identified as the author of this work.

All rights reserved. No part of this publication may be reproduced, stored in a retrieval system, or transmitted, in any form or by any means, electronic, mechanical, photocopying, recording or otherwise, without the prior written permission of the Publisher.

Printed in Poland, www.lfbookservices.co.uk

# Dedication

While the words that follow are mine, along with any errors, much of what appears in this book is the result of teamwork. The enjoyable task of producing the photographs is the obvious example, with the better images often showing me, because they were taken by Susannah. The collaboration strikes deeper than that though. I might cook out there, and often do, especially when it comes to baking bread or anything to do with fish, but the real culinary skills lie elsewhere in the partnership. Even beyond the warmth of the fire, and the preparation and creation of each anticipated meal, so much of what will be found between these covers is the product of that collaboration, from the planning undertaken before a camping trip even takes place, through the packing of kit and ingredients, to the collection of wood to fuel that all-important fire. It doesn't have to be like that of course. Each rewarding element of campfire cooking can be carried out perfectly successfully by the solo camper. I'm just extremely fortunate to be able to share it all.

## About the Author

Growing up on a farm, Tim has enjoyed an outdoor life since childhood. Subsequent work in forestry conservation and archaeology has added to an understanding and ever deeper love of the land. Camping has been a constant feature over the years, with tents pitched from sea level to mountain ridge, from the Mediterranean coast to Arctic Scandinavia.

Writing about fishing, hillwalking, canoeing, camp craft and camp cooking, the first of Tim's many magazine articles was published in 1990. He is a regular contributor to *Bushcraft and Survival Skills*, *Outdoor Adventure Guide* and *The Great Outdoors*, and has written on various subjects for magazines in Europe, Australia, Canada and the United States. His book, *Canoe Camping*, was published by Pesda Press in 2014.

Tim and Susannah met while camping and they have been pitching a tent at the end of a day's travel ever since. When not under canvas, Tim and Susannah live in Devon, England, midway between Dartmoor and the Atlantic coast.

# Contents

Dedication .................................................. 3
About the Author ....................................... 4
Contents ..................................................... 5

## Why Cook Over a Wood Fire ............... 7

## Kit ............................................................. 13
Carrying capacity ..................................... 16
Fire kit ....................................................... 21
Basic cooking kit ...................................... 35
More unusual cooking kit ....................... 47
Behind the scenes .................................... 54
Kit lists ...................................................... 55

## Fuel ............................................................ 61
How to prepare your wood ..................... 66
Kindling ..................................................... 74
Tinder ........................................................ 76

## How To Use a Wood Fire ..................... 79
Where to light a wood fire ...................... 79
Keeping pain free (or safety) .................. 83
First aid ..................................................... 84
Lighting ..................................................... 87
Finishing with your wood fire ................ 93
Problem solving ....................................... 95
Final fireside thoughts ............................ 97

## How To Cook Using a Wood Fire ........ 101
Pot and pan supports ............................... 103
Cooking ..................................................... 116
Reflector oven .......................................... 119
Dutch ovens .............................................. 121
Muurikka and fire bowls ......................... 123
After the meal .......................................... 124
Cleaning your pots and pans .................. 125

## What Food To Take And How To Take It .. 127
Ingredients ................................................ 127
Storage ...................................................... 136
How much food to take .......................... 137
Dehydrator ................................................ 138
Final thoughts .......................................... 138

## What To Cook ......................................... 141
Recipes ...................................................... 143
Bread ......................................................... 144
Little meals ............................................... 153
Big meals ................................................... 169
Puddings ................................................... 193

## Bibliography ........................................... 205

## Index ........................................................ 206

I'm certain the greatest camping satisfaction will come from preparing a meal over a wood fire.

Why Cook Over a Wood Fire

# Why Cook Over a Wood Fire

Heat radiates from a deep bed of glowing orange embers, both light and warmth enhanced by the advancing dusk. A lump of charcoal, ashimmer and bright, jumps slightly with a dull pop, before settling again amidst the downy grey ash at the fire's edge. Time for more fuel. Time for another stoke.

Almost as soon as the slim section of split beech meets the hot coals, tiny flames begin to shiver and creep along its flank. The log shakes just once, a small shower of sparks lifting into the cool evening air, before the superheated gasses take a proper grip, the fire once more ablaze. A hand reaches forward into the light, gripping a handle, sliding the battered steel pan at its end away from this resurgent heat. Inside, a fast rolling boil drops to a simmer.

So with our meal nearly ready, prepared over this satisfying blaze, it's time for an introduction. But rather than begin with the usual overview, and a description of what this book is about, I'm going to start from the other direction. Many might view cooking over a fire as a retrograde step, an odd and potentially uncomfortable rejection of easier, modern and more efficient methods. They will see only a questionable act, imposed either through circumstance and lack of options, or chosen because of some rose-tinted view of a better and more enlightened past. These are not my experiences, or the reasons that inspire me to collect firewood as mealtime approaches. As a result, this isn't a book about cooking over a wood fire as a result of necessity, being forced into campfire cooking in order to survive some

*Because it's enjoyable, deeply satisfying, versatile and efficient... and also a great way to cook good food.*

desperate and challenging situation, even if it might be a sensible response when other options are unavailable. It's not really about engaging with the past either, an attempt to reconnect with those millennia-long practices of our ancestors, however worthy that aim. Nor is it much concerned with the fact that wood-fired cooking has become rather fashionable of late, although I have to admit I'm very pleased more people are likely to be giving it a go as a result.

Instead, this book is about choosing to cook over a fire when camping because it's fun. It's about making the decision to use wood as a fuel to build that fire, because it's enjoyable, deeply satisfying, versatile and efficient, and because the whole process is environmentally sound and just about free. Importantly, for what otherwise would be the point, it's because cooking over a fire is also a great way to produce good food.

What's more, the whole process of campfire cooking really can be a lot easier than you might imagine, at least with a little guidance... and that's the reason for this book.

Of course, unless you were once in the Scouts or Guides, the chances are that preparing food over an open fire is going to be something completely new. For many, the concept of cooking in a camp at all will be a novel and slightly alarming prospect. For those who have already given it a go, the process is likely to have involved a bottle of gas. A pot sits on a stovetop. A knob is turned. The food inside is heated. Compared to the campfire, with its complex and alien contraptions, not least that worrying pile of burning wood, all this does seem reassuringly familiar. This book aims to show that with the right information and guidance, and the correct kit, cooking over what might at first seem a disconcerting wood fire can become just as natural.

True, at first glance, the alternative may seem very convenient, and in many ways it is. When one of those bottles of gas runs out, replacing it with another is almost effortless – assuming you have a replacement that is. Otherwise it's a trip in to town, or at least the nearest garage.

When Susannah and I need more fuel, we simply turn to the nearest copse or wood, even the beach stretched out before our tent. There, usually in a matter of only a minute or two, and collecting only a small amount of dead windfall or flotsam, we'll have a fresh supply. Unlike that gas though, our new heat source will be free.

In releasing its energy, and providing that useful heat, our wood fuel will also be clean. The carbon dioxide from that canister of gas was trapped below ground millions of years ago, until released again, that is, first by drilling, then by the burning of that fuel. The same rather troublesome gas from the donor tree was captured over only the last few decades, at most a century or two; carbon dioxide that the dead tree would have released anyway as it rotted away over the next few years. Nothing of additional concern is being added to our hard-pressed land or air.

Once a few meals have been prepared, the gas-fired camper is also left with a metal container. Depending on location, circumstance, and the attitude of the camper, this may or may not be recycled. At the end of our cooking sessions, once our meal is eaten, the pots, pans and dishes washed and packed away, Susannah and I have ash. With no effort, the remaining nutrients can be offered back to the local woodland straight away. If cooking over gas really is easier, and I have my doubts about that too, at what cost do we obtain that ease and simplicity.

Then there's that all-important matter of fun. And while I would far rather see someone spending time outside, cooking over whatever fuel they fancy, I'm certain the greatest camping satisfaction will come from preparing a meal over a wood fire. It's almost in our DNA. I mentioned just now that this book is not designed to revel in the past, but there's no denying an extremely rich heritage of cooking over wood that stretches back over many millennia in almost every culture. Only this week I camped with someone whose grandmother had cooked over wood, or at least peat, throughout her life. Just the slightly smoky taste of bread toasted over a fire takes her straight back to childhood.

That bottled gas.

A small shower of sparks lifts into the cool evening air.

Why Cook Over a Wood Fire

Heat radiates from a bed of glowing orange embers.

Of course that enjoyment can only really be experienced once a genuine confidence in the whole process is obtained. I hope that by the end of this book you will have gained the self-assurance needed to explore the countless benefits, culinary and aesthetic, to be had from cooking over a wood fire. I've even included some recipes.

For Susannah and myself, a wood fire is the normal heat source we employ to cook while camping. In our minds the two go together quite naturally, and we camp quite a bit. We've been doing it for a fair while too. We even met at an informal campsite, one where wood-fired cooking was the norm. This isn't to say that we always use wood. Local conditions, and even local regulations (see page 79 How To Use a Wood Fire), mean we can be required to use one of those bottles of gas. Some areas, for environmental or safety reasons, or simply to avoid interfering with other people's camping enjoyment, are just not suited to wood-fired cooking. Even so, we are fortunate to experience numerous opportunities every year to seek out those places where it is possible and allowed. In fact, it's a principle reason we choose to camp in these particular spots in the first place.

Those who have read about our travels before will know that much of our camping is carried out at the end of a canoe journey, and while this isn't the place to start extolling the many benefits of a canoe as a camping support vessel, this experience is relevant. Using such an excellent load carrier, Susannah and I are not really restricted in what we can transport into the wild. As a result, the cooking kit we take canoe camping, and the methods used around our campfire, can be translated directly to pretty much any situation in which you find yourself setting out in a self-propelled vehicle, whether a bicycle, kayak or rowing boat. In fact, whatever muscle-powered method you might choose to carry your kit into the wild.

Because so many of our canoe voyages take place at the end of a van drive, occasionally quite long van drives, the experiences accumulated on these journeys are also relevant to any situation where a motorised vehicle takes the strain. Many aspects of wood-fired camp cooking can change quite a bit with all the additional storage space offered by a van or truck. If you want them to change that is.

At the other end of the camping spectrum, I don't intend to forget the pedestrian. Although a large proportion of our camping is accompanied by a canoe, or carried out from the back of a van, we often camp as backpackers too. On these expeditions we also cook over a wood fire, or at least we do whenever possible. As a result, this guide will cover the alterations to kit and methods required to make the whole thing practical for anyone setting out with a well-stocked rucksack.

Mind you, while this book approaches wood-fired cooking from the perspective of the camper, there's absolutely no reason why the methods discussed in the following few chapters cannot be applied with equal success by anyone wishing to cook over a fire. It's not a requirement to have a tent pitched in the background. Whether you choose to prepare a meal in your back garden, at the beach, or anywhere else you can light a fire, the uplifting process is just the same.

No tent... just the enjoyment of a fondue on the beach, cooked over a wood fire.

Why Cook Over a Wood Fire

A well equipped canoe camping kitchen - kettle, casserole pot, fire irons, cutting board, knife, wooden spoon and wannigan, even an Indian travelling spice container.

# Kit

On any trip that takes us off the beaten track, the kit we choose to carry can have a profound impact on the experience. Or at least that's what all the outdoor magazines and guidebooks will try to tell us. The thing is, they're right.

Set out with the wrong equipment, particularly weighed down by too much of it, and our chance of achieving anything that approaches camping pleasure really is going to be reduced. Often forming the heavier element of any kit collection, and sometimes quite a bulky part, cooking gear can play a disproportionate role in that equation. This chapter is intended to help with those camp cooking kit decisions, particularly those surrounding cooking over an open fire.

It's true that some campers seem to relish a struggle out there, almost revelling in situations they may refer to in later accounts as an 'epic'. That's fine, but for the rest of us camping success is likely to be measured by the ease with which a comfortable temporary home can be created in the wild. While we might enjoy a challenge when it comes to attempting a particular dish for the first time, or trying out a new grilling method, even a new grill, it will also be the simplicity with which a meal can be prepared that is usually the gauge of cooking achievement, especially if that meal tastes good too.

Right from the start, there's an awful lot to be said for simplicity. We are going camping after all. So, whether you plan to head out into the wild with a 65 litre rucksack, a sixteen-foot canoe, or even a long wheelbase Land Rover, making the most of available cargo space is crucial. The art of leaving things behind, the right things of course, is

The sort of cooking kit we might take canoe camping. Clockwise from bottom left – washing up bowl, cloths, scourer, kitchen roll and 'clean everything' biodegradable liquid soap; cutting board, spatula and knife; frying pan and wooden spoon; stainless-steel pans (and handle); Kelly kettle; Primus kettle; fire irons and wire oven shelf. All we need to add is something to cut up some wood for fuel.

The cooking fire, its fuel, and the tools used to prepare it.

definitely one to be cultivated. While the value of a small and light load when filling that backpack should be obvious, even the 4x4 driver needs to be wary. In fact, one of the key dangers of camping while supported by a good load carrier, whether a van or even a canoe, is the temptation to add just another item or two... or three.

Of course kit simplicity needs to reflect an efficient minimalism. In short, and this isn't going to come as much of a surprise, we need stuff that actually works. Camp cooking kit made up from items that do their job properly, preferably more than one job, is vital. But how do we manage that?

If I state that a process of protracted field trial is the most likely way to best fulfil these twin goals of simplicity and function, you'll probably not be too surprised by that either. Tried and tested items inevitably possess the least chance of failing you at that inconvenient moment, in the middle of nowhere... when you're hungry.

Kit that has developed over years of intense trial will always be safer too. This is important. Any kitchen tends to witness a high proportion of the usual domestic mishaps and accidents. It's inevitable when you consider the profusion of sharp and hot materials at play. Take those activities outside, into the unfamiliar setting of a campsite, quite possibly a new campsite every night, and the risk of injury is bound to increase. The advantages of working with familiar implements and tools in these surroundings shouldn't be overlooked, especially when it comes to preparing firewood, and heating things over the burning results. Knowing without thinking how the handle of a pot of boiling water can be grasped most securely, the best angle to make that first saw cut into a length of driftwood, or recognising when the stability of a grill support is being pushed to unsafe limits, will all ensure that the chance of misfortune is kept to a minimum. Nothing spoils the fun of a night in the wild like a cut or burn, even a minor one. The implications of a more serious accident out there shouldn't need emphasising.

Each fresh site will have its own collection of unfamiliar dips, bumps, trip hazards and even overhead dangers. All this is inevitably going to push the whole process of camp cooking a little higher up any scale of risk. We'll talk more about the advantages of creating a familiar working environment later, but the benefits to your general wellbeing from a collection of familiar kit, and not too much of it, shouldn't be underestimated.

This isn't to say that we need to be too hard on ourselves. If you find a little spare packing space in your rucksack or kayak storage compartment, please feel free to use it, just use it carefully. And every once in a while, don't forget to take something new along with you. Unless an untried item of kit is taken out into the wild every now and again, how can you experiment? This sort experimentation is not only pleasurable, but by far the best way to improve your kit selection. Every year Susannah and I seem to find something that becomes an indispensible cooking item, often pushing aside an item of kit we didn't think could be bettered only the year before.

To a large extent, kit selection will be linked closely to a camper's chosen method of travel. This is hardly surprisingly. The lone backpacker will inevitably view kit options in a very different light to someone setting out on a camping trip in a large van. Then again, even someone with plenty of cargo haulage capacity may still prefer to keep things simple, and probably benefit from it. Conversely, the backpacker may be happy to shoulder the extra weight of some favourite item of kit, a particular tool or implement, despite its apparent bulk. I know a few seasoned backwoods travellers who never set off without a small axe strapped to their rucksack. In their view it is worth the extra weight and space.

The right kit also needs to match not only the available transport, or lack of it, but the character of the traveller, and their cooking abilities, style and aspirations. What might be considered a must-have item by one camper, won't even merit a second glance by another. Many people love the durability of a stainless steel or enamel mug for example, and while I usually veer towards campsite tradition, I've burnt my mouth often enough on these little monsters to abandon them in preference of something in plastic. I also prefer the feel of a carbon-steel knife for cooking duties, and the ease with which the blade will take a sharp edge. Others though will find the effort of keeping that blade rust free makes a stainless steel knife the only choice for them.

Inevitably the kit deliberations presented in the next few pages will tend to favour the choices Susannah and I make. This will extend to the way in which it is used too. I'm not troubled by this. It even makes a lot of sense to me. After many years of happy trial and occasional error, we're confident in the kit selections that have evolved, and confident in recommending them. I will try hard though not to present these choices exclusively. Other options will also be offered. Besides, we're still learning too.

Kit... it's all about choice.

To accompany the following suggestions, we've attempted to provide some of the background to our selection, even the reasons why we may have rejected certain pieces of kit. Advice on how best to put each item to use will be provided in subsequent chapters.

Almost inevitably, the following kit presentation and discussion will form a bit of a list. To break things up a little, and to make it easier to find the information you want, the catalogue is sub-divided. The first part will look at the kit needed to produce, look after and use your fire, while the second deals with the cookware itself, the pots, pans and other culinary odds and ends you might take away into the wild. But first, because they make such a difference to those choices, a quick look at those transport choices.

## Carrying capacity

Pulling in to the bank of a lively river in Arctic Finland, we hauled our canoe ashore, pitched our tent, and cooked a meal in a single pot over a simple support made from two lengths of angle iron (more on these later). As we reduced the sauce, water boiled for tea in a separate kettle. That saucepan and kettle... and those fire irons, formed pretty much the entirety of our cooking gear for that trip. Yes we also carried a bow saw and axe to cut wood for fuel, and the usual collection of knives and wooden spoons, but not much more.

The next day, a little further downriver, we pulled ashore again, this time to pick lingonberries. Tight alongside some rapids, slightly lacklustre at summer flow levels, we came across a small abandoned gravel quarry. Parked at one edge was one of the largest camper vans I've ever seen.

Fitted with Russian plates, this Mercedes Unimog looked as if it had been built to house a small village. To one side, between this lorry and the river, a very friendly couple had set out their camp kitchen. A good blaze crackled in a broad wrought iron trough. Pots and pans hung overhead on a hefty metal beam, arranged, ready for action, in descending size order, while below others already sat in play over the flames. Close by, beyond the table, chairs and a chainsaw, a large splitting axe leaned against an upturned section of sawn tree, surrounded by scattered split logs. They were obviously having as much fun as us, just expressed in a very different sort of way, made possible by the way they were travelling.

This short section summarises the kit carrying capabilities of some of those different ways, ranking them in a simple list.

**Vans, trucks and cars**

With images of that large Mercedes still fresh, there'll be not much surprise to find that top of the kit carrying pile comes anything fitted with wheels and an engine. While a large canoe might still manage to outperform a small car when it comes to lugging camping gear into the hills, the van, truck or 4x4 has the space to carry almost any kit you might wish into the wild. Even a pretty small car, depending on passenger numbers at least, could manage pretty much any cooking kit you might wish to take camping.

It's hard to beat a van when it comes to hauling camping gear.

Our canoe, loaded and ready to go.

## Canoe

With craft up to, and sometimes exceeding, 6m (20 feet) in length, and over 1m (3 feet) in width, providing carrying capacities measured in hundreds rather than tens of kilos, pretty much anything we might choose to take camping can be carried in a canoe too. Only the vast fire bowls or those wrought-iron cooking ranges of the van or 4x4 campers need be left behind. It's worth mentioning that campers in North America still occasionally use replicas of the great trading canoes of the 18th and 19th centuries. With teams of six or more paddlers, these can out-carry even many diesel powered trucks.

Even leaving these rarities aside, the canoe is always going to represent the biggest load carrier for the self-propelled camper. It was what they were built for after all. Unless you choose a large rowing boat that is, and I'll quietly slot these vessels in here too.

Cargo limits for a canoeist revolve around safety and back care. While your canoe may be able to carry almost anything, it can only do so on water. Should you plan to travel over lakes, fjords or sea lochs, or even many calmer rivers, this is fine. But where you might need to carry (or portage as canoeists call it) your kit from one lake to another, or around a waterfall or a long sequence of rapids, just remember that it is you, not your canoe, that will have to do the lugging. That Dutch oven you love to cook in may be best left at home. The other limit on cooking kit loads concerns safety. Pots and pans, not to mention stoves, don't float. While this is not the place to go into the methods of compensating for the problem, and it is possible through sensible packing and storage options, all this does need to be considered.

Where used for travel, rowing boats, depending on size, have roughly the same carrying qualities, and the same drawbacks.

Although not strictly self-propelled, I'll also mention sailing dinghies here. For a start, not being wildly keen on inflexible rules, I'm quite happy to include them, and besides, once you've experienced the effort needed to work one of these into a stiff breeze for a few miles, it would be hard to argue that muscle power, and sometimes a fair bit of grit, isn't required. Obviously, the loads that can be carried vary considerably depending on size and model.

## Kayak

For the kayak user, with some touring boats able to haul total loads (with the paddler) of anything up to around 180–200kg (400–440lb) the limits on potential kit are likely to revolve less around strict carrying capacity, and more on the size of the opening into the storage compartments. For structural strength, resistance to unwanted flooding, and narrow beams (widths), many kayaks have frustratingly small hatches. Care over weight distribution will also often limit what can be carried, perhaps even more so than with a canoe, where you can get at it all to make adjustments reasonably easily.

With tight, awkward and inflexible storage spaces, not to mention those small access hatches, it's also much easier to load a kayak, and a lot quicker, if you don't have to pack everything in tightly.

The hatch on this sea kayak is pretty standard, not very big, and a definite limiting factor in the kit that can be carried.

Our Moto Guzzi loaded for adventure, with not a lot of room for cooking kit.

Ben Gerard's bicycle, with all the storage capacity, and that's not a great deal, for his summer long tour from Belgium to northern Scandinavia.

Rucksacks need some very careful thought when it comes to what to fit in.

## Motorbike

With an engine in the mix, it might be assumed that a motorbike would be able to carry quite a bit of kit, and up to a point it can. That point is critical however, and needs to be recognised long before riding characteristics are compromised. Put simply, an overloaded motorbike can be a very unwieldy and dangerous thing.

Without going into the detail of that loading, which is really the subject for an altogether different book, the key to safe motorcycle touring lies in ensuring that kit is secure, and carried in the right place. Crucially, both these considerations are made a lot easier by keeping overall weights as low as possible. Depending on the machine in question, this is likely to be no more than about 30–40kg (65–85lb).

## Bicycle

When it comes to human-powered two-wheeled vehicles, all the concerns of the motorcyclist regarding weight, distribution and that all-important stability are just as valid. So while some touring cyclists, in the right conditions, may feel able to carry comparable kit loads, most will wish to pack far less. Once all the other camping gear is taken into account, only a couple of kilos (pounds), perhaps a maximum of 5kg (11lb) are likely to be available for anything to do with cooking.

## The rucksack

Then we have the backpacker. Free to roam at will, over land at least, but far more restricted than all other self-propelled campers when it comes to kit. With sensible total loads, depending on size, fitness and experience, ranging from around 10kg (22lb) to not much more than double that figure, cooking kit options are always going to be somewhat limited – although not, I'd stress, enough to limit the fun.

Once again, the weight available for the cooking kit once everything else is accounted for will fall considerably below that total, with perhaps only a couple of kilos available. Just my billy can and folding saw alone (wood-fire cooking backpack essentials in my book) weigh 0.8kg, or over 1½lbs.

# Fire kit

With the various carrying methods considered, we can turn to the kit you'll be hauling into the wild. As a fire is going to be required before any cooking can take place, let's look first at the hardware required to make lighting and tending that astonishing entity a pleasure.

## Matches

A while ago, quite a long while, humans managed to devise all manner of fascinating and ingenious ways to light a fire. Taking the time to learn some of these techniques, even putting them into practice every now and again, can be both fulfilling and useful. After all, you never know when you might need them. Thanks however to the chemist John Walker and his ever so useful ignition system stuck to the end of a small stick, you really don't need to. So while I might be able to produce a blaze employing friction, or by striking a chunk of high-carbon steel with a flint, and even choose to adopt these methods every now and then, I suspect that 95%... no make that 98% of our campfires begin their life with me striking a match.

To ensure that I can do this wherever and whenever I choose, I usually carry at least two boxes. One will be stored carefully in my shoulder bag or rucksack, stored in a dry bag, but as there's a chance, albeit a small one, that I might be separated from these mini kitbags out there, another box will lurk in its own protective cover in a coat pocket. When travelling by canoe it's not unusual for Susannah and me to carry perhaps two or three extra little cardboard containers, each stored inside either a dry bag, or in one of those clip-shut plastic food boxes. Whether travelling by kayak, bicycle or donkey, you should have space to do the same.

These dry bags and boxes, each with their precious load, will then be secreted at several points throughout our camping kit, tucked into various different holdalls or rucksacks. Belt and braces? Maybe, but this precaution will suddenly seem ever so sensible should you ever be unfortunate enough to find yourself in a scrape in

Matches, stored in two different watertight containers.

*My fire-steel, along with its dry bag, and yet another box of matches.*

*A telescopic blowpipe, and a rough idea of size in comparison with my reindeer skin tinder bag.*

which only one bag of kit survives. Knowing that somewhere deep inside that sole container rests a guaranteed way to light a fire and heat some food, can be very reassuring. Let's also hope there's something to eat in that bag too.

## Other lighting methods

While I may not use it often, I also carry a modern fire-steel set into the wild – always. Made, appropriately enough, by the Swedish company Light My Fire, this simple piece of kit offers a guaranteed fire-lighting method should others fail due to loss or damage. All I need do is scrape the fancy magnesium alloy with the attached steel tang, and this wonderful little tool produces a great shower of very hot tinder-igniting sparks.

Considering all those dry bags and waterproof clip-boxes, it might be unlikely that our ample match collection should ever experience a soaking, but if it should, I'll still be able to rely on that fire-steel to provide something orange and warm that dances bright around a bundle of twigs.

Of course if it makes you feel happier to know you have a gas lighter ready and waiting in a jacket pocket, then please feel free to carry it. In the end, a lit fire is the crucial thing, not the manner in which you achieve it.

While discussing fire lighting kit, I'll also take the opportunity to mention a small and easily portable item that can help. A telescopic blowpipe is just a graduated pipe in sections. You simply blow in at the broad end, and the thin end of the pipe puts a concentrated jet of air exactly where it's needed amongst any glowing bits, while keeping eyebrows, fringes, plaits and beards well away from the results of success. This can be a great help with those sometimes reluctant stages early in the life of a fire, but also when you need to kick a little verve back into an unenthusiastic or ignored fire. Sometimes called pocket bellows, which I think is rather misleading as your lungs do all the work, good ones can be bought purpose made. Mine is a section of old car aerial.

And because it merits a mention as early as possible, especially once a lit fire is discussed, a first aid kit is always going to be a positive addition to any campfire cooks' kit collection. This is even more useful if it's represented by a selection designed especially for outdoor use, and put together to cater for the number of people in your camping party.

### Tinder box, or bag

We can return to the matter of what to put in it later, but carrying some form of tinder box or bag with you will make the firelighting process so much easier and more enjoyable, especially when faced, late in the day, with a tinder barren site. In the end, most campsites will possess something useful nearby, a few tufts of dry grass, a bank of dead leaves, or best of all a birch tree with a few sheets of papery bark fluttering in the breeze... but not always.

*A first aid kit, with one of the reasons you might need it.*

The key to the right container is exactly the same as the one carrying your match collection – its waterproofness. Admittedly my favourite tinder, birch bark, works perfectly well when damp. As a result, I keep my supply in a reindeer leather bag, the sort usually sold as coffee bags. For nearly all other tinders, something more water resistant is required. A clip-lock plastic box is ideal, or even an old tobacco tin for those with more traditional leanings. Whatever the choice, keep this container either with you, or in the bag closest to your side.

### Axes, saws and other cutting tools

Midway through the third week of a visit to Arctic Scandinavia, having already camped on three islands, both banks of a river and a stunning section of wooded coast, a rather interesting fact suddenly struck me. Breaking a few lengths of driftwood over my knee, it was only as I encountered a particularly stubborn plank, and on turning to locate the bag carrying our bow-saw, that I realised I hadn't yet pulled this tool out. In fact, during the course of the whole trip, and while preparing a couple of dozen meals in a reasonable selection of varied sites, I hadn't employed either my axe or folding saw either. I hadn't even unsheathed my knife. Our fire had been fed, perfectly adequately, by fuel collected and broken up for use by hand. Pause for thought.

Breaking firewood by hand on an Arctic Scandinavian evening.

The most obvious conclusion is that despite having written reams in the past about the careful selection and use of various campfire supporting bladed implements, I may have been rather overstating the issue. Those happy tool-free weeks would seem to suggest so anyway. Then again, looking at this scenario more closely, perhaps a rather more complex message is illustrated.

In perfect conditions, by which I mean the glorious and almost untouched wilderness woodland of northern Sweden, surrounded by tight-packed and virtually unvisited forest, adequate fuel lies all about, quite literally, for the picking. Decent dead wood is scattered everywhere, in any size. If the piece you have just selected is too big to break by hand, you can simply drop it and look for another that isn't.

You don't even need to travel as far as Arctic Scandinavia to find this pleasant and easy-going situation. On reflection, I realise we've camped many a time in Scotland where all I've used to collect and prepare firewood is my bare hands. Admittedly, this is helped by a confident belief, based on a fair bit of experience, that efficient cooking fires can be fed perfectly adequately, even best fed, with really quite insubstantial pieces of wood, and we'll return to this important point later.

But what about those situations where the supply of even this small stuff is more limited, perhaps where other campers have already visited the area before you? Even on that Norwegian coast, at about 69° north, people had camped there already, quite often it would seem. The woodland, rich and untouched as it first appeared, was actually picked pretty bare. This wasn't a problem of course. Beaches are almost always rich in timber flotsam, and the little shingle bay below our tent was no different, but I did need help in order to break those large washed up pieces down to a usable size. It was at that moment that I was very thankful for that saw, ignored as it had been up to that point. Put simply, it would have been pretty difficult to cook without it.

Which leads to another interesting point, illustrated by this now carefully picked over example. When I did eventually need to cut some wood, I turned first for a saw.

**Saws**

Much as many of us might relish the image of ourselves striding into the nearest forest in search of fuel, a trusty axe propped casually over one shoulder, the saw is often the better choice for the wood-fire using camper. Not only are saws very versatile, but in the hands of anyone but an expert, they are invariably much safer. A poorly handled saw can still cause an uncomfortable injury, but nothing compared to the results of a misplaced axe swing.

Saws come in all shapes and sizes, almost all of which, depending on travel methods at least, are perfectly usable. Some campers even take a standard carpenter's saw into the wild, and where I've given this a go myself I've been surprised by just how handy they can be. When most outdoor types think of these tools though, it will be a bow saw that springs to mind.

Today, these saws usually come in one of three standard blade lengths – 52.5cm (21 inch), 60cm (24 inch) or 75.9cm (30 inch) – with the shortest often held in a triangular fame. In my experience the best bow saws are made in Sweden. Wherever your saw comes from, make sure it arrives fitted with a plastic clip-on blade guard.

A bow saw can be just as useful as an axe, possibly more so.

Kit 25

Unless you have plans for some serious timber reduction out there, those bow saws fitted with the largest blades are probably best ignored. If nothing else, they really do take up quite a bit of room, even if you're using a large vehicle to carry your camping load. For canoe camping use I definitely prefer the 60cm (24 inch) version, which is big enough for almost all jobs, and easy to handle. For anyone without too much concern for storage space, I'd certainly recommend this middle-sized saw. The 52.5cm (21 inch) models will probably be compact enough, just, for a kayaker.

**Folding saws**

When space becomes a premium, even these bow saws are a little unwieldy. Fortunately, other bow saw options exist, and folding or collapsible versions are readily available. For those with an eye for traditional aesthetics, wooden framed versions can be found easily enough. Not only do they look good, these saws work very well too. But for the weight conscious traveller such as the kayaker or cyclist, a folding aluminium saw is almost certainly a much better bet. The version designed by the Minnesotan Bob Dustrude (I suspect he calls it a folding buck saw) is a gem. Light and compact when closed up, and simple to assemble, it feels almost as sturdy as a conventional fixed model in use.

The Dustrude folding saw, against a Welsh hedge.

Then there are small folding saws, often designed originally for pruning. These can be obtained from a variety of sources, and good ones come not only from Sweden, but also Germany or Japan. I almost never leave home without one, and for almost all campfire feeding tasks, at least those fires built for cooking, these small but very effective saws will do just fine. Any backpacker intending to cook over wood should probably consider a small folding saw like this as an essential kit item, perhaps made by Stihl, Silky or Bahco.

My small Stihl folding saw. It travels almost everywhere with me.

*Axes*

Of course, if space and carrying capabilities allow, an axe certainly has its place, and while it may be pulled from its bag only rarely, when it is needed it can make a huge difference. So which axe?

My first suggestion is simple. However you intend to travel, you almost certainly don't need what's commonly referred to in North America and Britain as a felling axe. These job-specific tools (the hint's in the name) are far too heavy in the head, and too long in the shaft for convenient camp use. Besides, unless you are an experienced axe user, any felling or limb cutting is probably best approached with something less ungainly anyway.

An example of a hand-forged Scandinavian hatchet, this one made by Husqvarna.

For many, a small axe, often referred to as a hatchet, with a head weight of just under 0.5kg (1lb) and a handle length of around 35cm (or 13 inches) will do. Easy to use single handed, something like the Husqvarna hatchet in the photo can also be wielded with two hands as well – just. Not surprisingly, if an axe is a must, but space and carrying capacity is limited, this size is the one for you.

For more controlled double-handed use, and usually still light enough for most people to manage with one hand, an axe with a handle of approximately 50cm (or 19 inches) in length and head weight of around 0.75kg (1.5lb) offers a more versatile tool. An axe of this size, and the Gränsfors Bruks Small Forest Axe is a good example, allows other cutting tasks to be undertaken easily as confidence in handling grows. I know quite a few bushcraft backpackers who carry one of these.

There is also another advantage to an axe with a longer handle – it is invariably safer than one fitted with a shorter version, the head of a wayward axe with a longer helve being more likely to hit the ground than you.

A good axe – The Gränsfors Scandinavian Forest Axe.

For the record, and as photographs show it, I usually use a Gränsfors Bruks Scandinavian Forest Axe. With a 65cm (25 inches) handle, and a head weighing around 1kg (2lb), this is quite a big axe. Despite its size though, and an ability to

Kit 27

An old 'Kent' pattern axe, and the sort of thing you can still pick up at a car boot sale, often at little cost.

manage smaller scale felling with ease, it is still light and small enough for me to use with one hand when the situation demands. Importantly, when we use it, our canoe can carry the weight.

In search of a reasonable axe, and without going into details which may start to sound like something close to a gripe, be a little wary of bargains. Many of the models offered in general hardware stores or tool merchants these days really aren't very impressive. Poorly designed and badly made, often from sub-standard materials, they're rarely worth even the sometimes fairly modest price. At the other end of the spectrum you then have a clutch of specialist companies such as Wetterlings, Hultafors or Gränsfors, that offer some simply stunning axes. These do come at a price mind you, albeit a justified one when you consider the result. If you do want a decent Swedish hand-forged axe, but also need to take care of the pennies, take a look at the Husqvarna range. These are very reasonably priced, and I have a hunch they're made by one of those illustrious makers anyway.

There is still another alternative however. If you wander about a car-boot sale or rural junk shop you can often find something from one of the many now defunct axe manufacturers. Most countries were once blessed with a string of companies producing quality hand tools at a reasonable cost. In Britain, the makers Elwell, Brades and Gilpin, even Spear and Jackson in their earlier years, spring to mind. Each made some very fine axes in their day. These can often be picked up in reasonable condition from a market stall or bric-a-brac store for just a few pounds. Fairly shoddy looking examples may set you back even less. Relatively little effort or time is usually needed to bring them back into working order. At worst, the outlay will be no more than the cost of a new handle and some elbow grease.

One final comment, if you do decide to purchase new. Any good axe maker will provide this tool with a leather cover (sheath) to clip over the head. An essential item, to protect you, your belongings, and the blade.

### *Knives*

When it comes to the wood-fired camp kitchen, a knife is indispensable. A huge range of duties can be accomplished around the fire with a decent blade, but two key tasks will be encountered; the cooking itself and the splitting of fuel.

The immediate problem is that these two jobs are not easily managed by a single blade. Anything fine enough for easy slicing of food will inevitably be too delicate for many wood preparation tasks, while a hefty woodsman's knife, often with a pretty sturdy blade, is equally unsuited to many cooking duties, certainly anything as delicate as filleting or fine paring.

An obvious solution to this knife conundrum is to carry two, one kept for the kitchen, the other reserved specifically for the fire. It's certainly my choice, and I carry an old Sabatier paring knife for food preparation (well, it's what it was made for after all) and a dedicated bushcraft knife to cut and split wood (for the same reasons).

For the backpacker there may not be much choice though, weight issues dictating that a single knife will have to cater for both cooking duties and wood reduction. That's quite a lot to ask.

One approach, and a very good one, would be to carry a bushcraft style knife, but one with a relatively thin blade, say less than 2.5mm (3/32 inch) in width. This blade should be fine enough for most cooking, yet still have the strength to split most of the wood you might take on. Remember that as a backpacker the vast majority of any wood-cutting will be undertaken only to feed a fire anyway.

For lightweight travellers, many of whom will certainly not relish the effort or difficulty involved in carrying an axe, a suitable knife will do the job perfectly well, only in a much smaller and lighter package. Paired with a folding pruning saw and almost any timber reduction task, at least those needed to feed a cooking fire can be managed. The methods employed will be looked at in detail later, but for now it's a matter of identifying and locating the right tool for the task, that suitable knife.

My Orford Woodlander knife.

A Finnish Puukko.

The job is actually quite easy. The growing enthusiasm for what is now almost universally called bushcraft has encouraged something of a rather miraculous renaissance in knife production. This seems to be particularly evident where I live here in Britain. A growing number of knife-makers are rejuvenating the old skills, producing some stunning working knives in the process. Some of these tools can be quite pricey, justifiably so, but there are also some surprisingly good examples made in larger numbers for a fair bit less. The best bet is to look at few articles, reviews and adverts in specialist bushcraft magazines.

As a basic guide, the better knives for the job will have a blade of about 10–13cm (4–5 inches) in length in what is called a full-tanged style. This means that the steel of the blade continues, full width, right through to the end of the handle. With either wood or artificial handle grips (scales) riveted directly to this one-piece bar of metal, the resultant knife is extremely strong. It will need to be, as wood splitting is particularly demanding, and the death-knell for many sub-standard knives in the wild. The blade can be made from either stainless or carbon steel, and ideally needs to be at least 2.5mm ($3/32$ inch) thick.

My favourite bushcraft knife was made by Ben Orford. For those interested in such details, it was forged from 01 high carbon tool steel, hardened to about 58 Rockwell. The blade is 10cm (4 inches) long and 3.5mm ($1/8$ inch) thick, sharpened with what is called a classic Scandi flat grind. Lois Orford produced the leather sheath that manages the tricky balance of protecting the knife and ensuring it can never fall out, while always being easily removed when needed.

The only other type of knife I feel happy with is a Scandinavian style forest knife. These have only what is called a narrow, stick or spear-tanged handle, in which the blade continues, hidden, up through the centre of the handle, but the good ones are up to the task. The famous Swedish company Mora make some excellent basic knives at a very reasonable cost. Wood Jewel and Caastrom in Finland produce traditional Puukko style knives that are also excellent value for money.

***Secateurs and pruners***

Many wood burning campers carry secateurs. Others pack larger cutting tools that people often refer to as either pruners or loppers. Many swear by them, and I have responded to their enthusiasm by giving them a go.

My conclusions are that secateurs are great in the garden, where you're often dealing with pliable green wood that can sometimes be very resistant to manual attack. However the dry stuff the camper is looking to burn, at least in the diameter secateurs can deal with, can just as easily be broken by hand. Mind you, that's just what works for me.

I have to admit though that a good pair of loppers can be very helpful, as they have the ability to cut their way through stuff that is usually to big to take on manually. The best examples, not surprisingly, need to be pretty tough, and can even manage branches up to 3cm (1½ inches) across.

A good pair of loppers, in use.

## Portable stoves

And so to the fire itself.

Where conditions and legislation allow, Susannah and I definitely prefer to work with a standard open fire, but then these two basic criteria are not always met. This is where something designed to keep the fire enclosed within some form of container or stove can make all the difference. Small stoves are not only tidier, with much less risk of the fire escaping; they are also extremely efficient. Keeping not only the fuel, but also much of the resultant heat in one enclosed space means that often surprisingly little wood is needed to bring a set of ingredients to edible perfection. For the backpacker in particular, wishing to cook over a wood fire, some sort of compact stove can make all the difference, even where an open fire is welcome.

Our portable stove in use on a Cornish beach.

A whole range of tiny devices, usually built from stainless steel, are available. Many are designed to store flat, either folding or built from interlocking sheets. For obvious reasons these are likely to best suit the backpacker. As a result of understandable attempts to keep these stoves as light as possible, they can sometimes be rather flimsy, and occasionally slightly precarious. If space allows, something built in one solid piece can be a better option.

I have to admit to relatively limited experience with these purpose-built mini stoves – not because I don't like to cook over a small, contained fire, but because, some years ago now, I built my own. As this simple homemade stove not only worked, but continues to do so years later, I keep using it. Made from a short connecting section of 7-inch stainless-steel chimney flue, just 12 cuts, 6 slight folds and a little filing to remove sharp edges were needed to create something functional. I hope the accompanying photos provide enough information for anyone wishing to build their own. I will admit, that at a little over 0.9kg (2lb) in weight, and standing 25cm (10 inches) high, it is a touch on the hefty side for easy backpacking use.

Our portable stove, ready for action.

## Fire bowls and griddle pans (or Muurikka)

Usually built in wrought iron or pressed steel, a whole swathe of shallow bowls, in a wide range of sizes, fall into the fire bowl and griddle pan bracket. This creates a slight problem, but only for me.

In many ways it would be much easier to make a distinction between the two, between the fire bowls and the griddle pan or Muurikka (like many outdoor cooks I tend to refer to all griddle pans by the name of the Finnish company that popularised them), but there is a distinct crossover. So while this makes life a little tricky for a campfire cooking writer trying to pigeonhole things neatly, it does produce some very useful versatility for the outdoor cooking reader.

Some particularly big bowls, often with diameters approaching 1m (3 feet), and depths of 20–25cm (8–10 inches) are very definitively designed to hold only a fire.

The base of the stove, showing the flaps bent in to hold fuel away from the air inlets.

Kit 33

A particularly big fire bowl, with a large Muurikka waiting to be used.

A fire bowl awaiting its star role in an Austrian lakeside barbecue.

With their relatively high sides, these have the advantage of containing that burning wood and resultant ash neatly and safely, while also keeping that fire off the ground, avoiding any damage. For this reason, they are very popular in countries or areas like Finland, where to reduce the risk of forest fires, open cooking fires on the ground are often not allowed in the wild. Not surprisingly, you really need something with an engine to take one of these bowls camping.

At the other end of the spectrum, some of the smaller Muurikka, or griddle pans, are meant only for cooking. These shallow steel pans, usually with removable legs, sit over a fire, and can be used to fry, sauté, boil and dry roast all manner of meals and ingredients. For example, both Muurikka and the German company Petromax make a griddle pan of about 35cm (15 inches) in diameter.

Both companies also make a pan measuring about 48cm (19 inches) across, and this is where the division between fire bowl and Muurikka starts to become a little fuzzy. Because while these pans are great to cook on, they are also designed to carry the heat source. In fact, both Muurikka and Petromax promote the use of two pans, one to hold a fire, the other propped on top, in which to cook. This system is not only versatile and simple, but meets those Finnish restrictions. The largest Muurikka, at around 58cm (24 inches) in diameter, while making an excellent griddle pan for cooking, is also an ideal fire bowl. Many Finnish outdoor cooks use one of the large Muurikka to hold the fire that heats food in a slightly smaller one above. Others will pitch a steel tripod over the bowl to hold a cooking vessel, or even use fire irons, discussed soon.

Of course, with even the smallest Muurikka weighing nearly 4kg (about 8½lbs), these griddle pans are never going to appeal to a backpacker. For the same reason, even those using a bike or kayak are unlikely to succumb to their otherwise obvious charms. Only a canoe, and a relatively large one at that, will be suitable to carry one of these into the wild, and many canoe campers do take the small or medium sized models.

# Basic cooking kit

## Pot support systems

### *Fire irons*

There are almost as many ways to hold your pots and pans in place over a fire as there are camp cooks, and we'll discuss a collection of the most commonly employed methods in the next chapter. However, the props we use more than any other to support a pot or pan are our fire irons. I'd be pretty sad if I had to set out without them.

For many years I forgot all about the simple lengths of steel I'd propped over the embers as a youngster. I'm not even sure who taught me to use them originally, but was intrigued a while back to find Horace Kephart referring to them in his 1917 book 'Camping and Woodcraft'. He suggested employing two pieces of flat steel, measuring 24 x 1½ x 1⅛ inches, informing his readers confidently that 'any blacksmith will cut them for you in a minute'. Sadly the village blacksmith is a rather rare find these days, and besides I'm equally certain I've improved on even this very simple design.

When I came to search through a pile of metal offcuts, looking of something suitable to put this long forgotten system back into use, I discovered two lengths of angle iron, the mild steel about 3mm (roughly ⅛ inch) thick and 20mm (¾ inch) across each flat (a standard angle iron size). I think they once formed part of a small trailer. As found, these were just under 70cm (28 inches) long, so that's what I used. A fair bit of action since suggests that length was about right.

Propped on a pair of suitable stones, these irons provide excellent support for one, two or even three pots. If one frying pan or saucepan is smaller than the other, or you want to boil a kettle, all you have to do is push the irons closer together at one end. Should you need to grill something an old wire cooker shelf can be rested on top.

Our fire irons on a Swedish beach, providing a stable platform for a kettle.

And at the edge of a Swedish lake, supporting a kettle and saucepan.

Kit 35

Our oven shelf, in use over the fire irons to grill a perch.

Made of angle iron, these fire irons don't buckle or bend in the heat (as Kephart admits his flat bars had a tendency to do, and my original round steel rods certainly did). When not in use over the fire, they make a very good safety barrier, driven into the ground in the tent between our wood burning stove and the sleeping area. What's more, although I've fortunately not yet had call to try, I reckon they'd make pretty useful splints if a tent pole or the like ever needed mending.

These fire irons are also very easy to transport, nestled one inside the other, wrapped in an old canvas offcut, and slipped into our Mountain Equipment kitchen holdall. One slight drawback is that they can be a little sooty (as I've just proved once again by measuring them for this discussion). They are also rather too heavy for backpackers or cyclists, although a kayak will probably manage. Our canoe certainly doesn't seem to notice them.

I suspect it was one of the many former army officers found in retirement around the southern edge of Salisbury Plain who first introduced me to fire irons. Perhaps they'd read Kephart. Whoever it was has my gratitude, and I did at least remember this particular gem – eventually.

As they do a reasonable job in a pinch, it's worth mentioning that a pair of steel road pins, the sort used to hold up plastic orange fencing at the side of roadworks (or archaeological excavations), make half-decent fire irons when angle iron isn't available. They also have the advantage of being quite long, cheap and easy to get hold of although, on the down side, they have a tendency to warp and bend in the heat.

One idea that has rattled around my head for quite a while now is some form of super fire irons, designed to be light enough for backpacking use. Aluminium would possibly do the trick, or even titanium? I suspect that cost would be the main prohibiting factor for the latter.

### Grill

For grilling over a wood fire, we've long carried an old wire oven shelf. Being chromed it is easy to clean, and just slips over the fire irons.

These shelves can also be employed successfully on their own and we've managed perfectly happily, occasionally for quite long periods of time, using a largish one as our only form of camping pot support. Small lightweight versions also work well, and I've known backpackers carry a wire shelf from the oven grill pan with great success. These are light but strong, and can carry out a decent pot supporting role, propped on stones. As any of these shelves will become pretty grimy as soon as they are used, so some form of bag, even just a plastic carrier bag, will save the rest of your kit from developing a uniform greasy carbon layer.

### Folding trivet

While the fire irons I've just mentioned are really just a bit too heavy and bulky for the pedestrian camper to consider lugging around, at least until those perhaps mythical titanium versions are available, a folding trivet shouldn't be. These are available from a number of specialist outlets, and a few dedicated bushcraft blacksmiths also make collapsible versions. They probably offer the easiest way for a leg-powered traveller to cook easily over a campfire.

A good set should fold flat or break down into a package not much wider or deeper than a plate. Some of the specialist items, made of lightweight steel, weigh surprisingly little. Once set up, they need to be stable of course, and strong enough to hold a saucepan of stew.

The only real drawback of a trivet, and it's not much of a problem, is they are rarely big enough to carry more than one pan.

### Kit for other support systems

If a very lightweight grill shelf or folding trivet is still too much weight, the backpacker will probably need to look either to the hedgerow or coppice to provide support systems for any pot or pan. Here the raw materials needed to build a range of wayside supports, including the tripod and cantilever or camp crane, can be found afresh each evening. The methods and techniques for building and using

A collapsible trivet, made by our daughter Miranda. Hand forged in iron, this particular example is perhaps not the lightweight option a backpacker is looking for.

My Sabatier paring knife.

A well-used Opinel.

these structures, and others, will be discussed later in the chapter How To Cook Using a Wood Fire, but here we just need to mention the additional kit items that the pedestrian camper, or other lightweight traveller such as a cyclist or kayaker, will want to add to their load to make these systems function. Fortunately, this need comprise no more than a metre or two of stout cord for lashing staves, a couple of lightweight wire hooks (I use sections of old wire clothes hangers) and a metre or so of light chain. For this last item, I employ a section of chromed lavatory pull chain.

**Knives**

We've mentioned knives for fuel provision, and while it's perfectly reasonable to carry just one, designed to cover all tasks, it is often best, for health and practicality, to have a dedicated cutting implement for cooking.

I've mentioned our old Sabatier paring knife already. As this was created as a specialist cooking implement, it's not surprising that it does the job extremely well (and it weighs very little). When it comes to cooking, you can't really go wrong with something plucked from the kitchen.

One particular knife that doesn't come from the kitchen, but deserves a mention at this point is the French Opinel. This masterpiece of design is still produced by the Opinel family. It is simple, cheap, efficient, relatively light and, because it folds, is small enough to store easily. It can also be locked open, saving fingers, and turning it into something that is almost as useful as a fixed blade tool. The perfectly decent carbon-steel blade is also quite thin, making the Opinel a great emergency kitchen knife. The fine blade also complements the stronger and broader version on my fixed knife. Produced in a range of numbered sizes, I've always chosen a number 8. If memory serves right, I may have used pocket money to buy my first, in Brittany, when I was about the same age. The only problem with an Opinel in the camp kitchen is the difficulty in cleaning food residues from the blade slot in the handle. Not much of an issue with spinach or seaweed. Something to have rather more concern about when cooking fish or chicken.

Although not strictly for cooking, a Swiss-army knife is always worth considering if you have the space. With a bottle opener, and especially a tin opener, usually part of the repertoire of built in tools, these knives can represent either a useful backup, or fulfil the primary role when it comes to getting into food containers. They even have a useful standby blade, should your main knife prove hard to find.

**Cutting board**

While far from essential, a decent board for chopping and preparing food does make life much easier. Mind you, should the term board conjure up worrying images of a hefty chunk of wood, we carry a fairly large (almost A3), but very thin and light board, made of hard tough plastic. More of a sheet really, and highly recommended.

Ours weighs just 190gms (7oz), and for our usual canoe camping, this is no problem whatsoever. Although probably just about light enough to carry on your back, there are smaller versions, and I'd suggest an A5-sized plastic sheet would more than make up for its tiny weight when it comes to chopping onions in the evening.

More of a sheet really.

Kit  39

Our tiniest frying pan; ideal for the backpacker.

Our black iron frying pan in Sweden.

**Frying pan**

Not really an easy option for anyone letting Shank's Pony take the strain, but for all other campers, unless you intend to travel very light, a frying pan can be extremely useful.

For our canoe and van camping expeditions we carry a black iron pan. This has quite deep sides, and can be used for all sorts of cooking tasks other than just frying. These basic pans are great for the traditional look and fine if you are used to them and know how to season the steel and keep it all in top order, but more modern options may well suit most people rather better.

With this thought in mind, non-stick aluminium versions make for a lighter option, the smaller ones suitable for kayak haulage. If you really want to carry one on foot, there are some really tiny examples, usually with a folding wire handle. These are often designed to double up as lids for lightweight aluminium pots.

## Billy can

Much of the kit discussed here, due to weight or bulk, is appropriate only for the vehicle-supported camper, but not the billy can. This little pot, preferably with a lid, is a campfire cooking backpacker's mainstay. Whether hung from a tripod, a cantilever arm setup, propped on a mini-stove or even on some form of lightweight fire irons or griddle, the billy will allow you to rustle up a meal efficiently. If you choose not to carry a kettle, water can be boiled in it easily, and you can even drink the resultant brew straight from your can if you wish to leave a mug from your kit too.

Bare steel, enamelled tin and aluminium versions are all available, and perfectly functional. Even frighteningly expensive but extremely light titanium versions can be found, and for anyone keen to keep that pack weight down they're certainly worth consideration, despite the cost. I prefer stainless steel. This is pretty light, and certainly very tough for its weight. It's also easy to clean (an important consideration when cooking on a campfire), and for someone like me that just doesn't quite trust bare aluminium (not sure why, it just smells wrong) a stainless steel billy represents the perfect lightweight campfire cook's companion.

My favourite billy cans are made by the Thai company Zebra. For the lone backpacker, I'd suggest the 12cm version of what they call the Auto Lock Pot. The 14cm or 16cm cans are perfect for a larger group, or someone with a canoe or van. These pots come with a robust folding handle, a good lid, and an internal tray (for ice in their intended use as a food carrier in Thailand), which I discard, along with the plastic lid clips.

## Kettle

Even a backpacker might consider a separate kettle, perhaps made of titanium, and doubling up as a mug. It's often good to follow a meal with a tea or coffee, and it's never much fun to have to clean the remains of your stew from your billy can before making a brew.

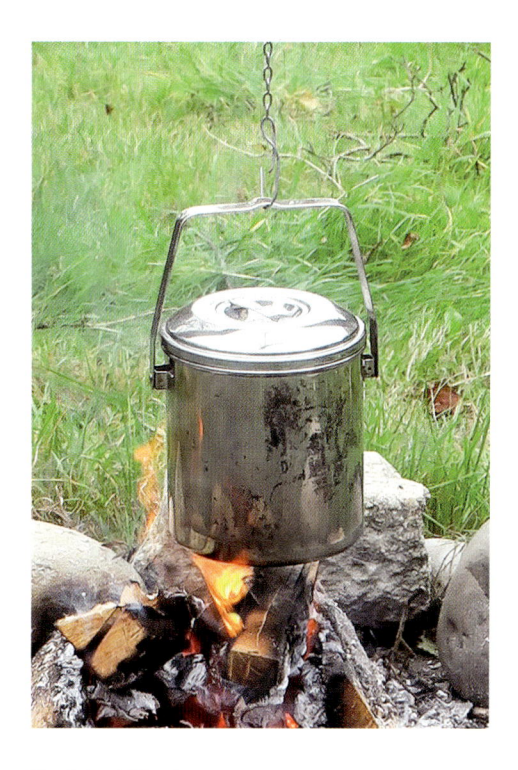

The Zebra billy can.

A Primus kettle.

Our Kelly Kettle in use on the Spanish coast.

For the vehicle assisted camper, and for the same reason, something larger is almost essential, and I do like the anodised aluminium kettles made by Primus (anodised aluminium doesn't smell strange). If you can find an old one, they're beautifully made.

At this point I will also mention Kelly Kettles. I have lugged one of these around in a rucksack, and I'd probably do it again because I like them so much. I'd always take one along when I don't have to carry everything myself.

It might be argued that if you have a fire going you may as well just use a standard kettle, and I'd agree. It's those frequent occasions when a hot drink hovers somewhere between pleasant and life saving, and a fire isn't already lit, that they come into their own. Even if you are extremely good at lighting a standard fire, you're not likely to produce boiling water at anywhere near the speed of a Kelly Kettle, or with such little fuel. These little camping stars even work well in a stiff breeze.

**Saucepans**

This is where size and weight really do need to be considered, both in relation to travel methods and personal cooking requirements. Saucepans are certainly very useful, but how many, and in what material?

Plain steel or enamel pots are cheap and fairly cheerful, but once again stainless steel provides what I believe represents the best of both worlds, being pretty tough, fairly light, and very easy to look after. We've carried a nesting set of three MSR pots around with us for years, and despite being fairly battered now, they still work just as well as ever. These pans have one of those drilled aluminium hinged grips, looking like a spare part from a WWI biplane, designed to allow you to pick up and move your handle-less pots. With a little practice, the system works well; you just need to be very careful not to mislay that grabber. Just to be on the safe side, as they are rather important, we carry two in our kit, one stored safely in our food box, the other nestled inside the inner pot. As it has a tendency to rattle around irritatingly when stored in there, we wrap it in a plastic shopping bag or two, one of which is often used to carry our cooking rubbish out from the wild.

For our canoe camping trips, and in addition to our Primus kettle, we take all three of these saucepans. When backpacking, and that's assuming we don't take the billy can, just the one. In brief, when using a rucksack, it's a kettle and one pan. To keep weight down for the leg-powered camper, or for anyone else with haulage concerns, titanium is worth mentioning again as it is extremely light and tough. You do pay the price though, literally.

There are other options however, at least for the camper with wheels or a hull to take the strain. I want to stress this because campers can often become rather too hung up by the idea of using only dedicated camping gear. This makes every sense when space and carrying strength is limited. If you are travelling by bicycle, then please pick something lightweight from the camping shop cooking rail. On the other hand, if you have a van, truck or canoe waiting to haul you and your kit away from humanity's bustle, why not consider packing a pan or two from your kitchen. Something with a good solid base is designed for efficient even cooking after all.

Our largest MSR pan, with the grab-handle to the side.

If you can carry it easily, and you like to cook with it, why not take that saucepan along. When we camp with a canoe, and where we don't expect to carry (portage) our kit over any distance, we often take an old French cast-iron pot.

### Tin foil

A roll of tin foil, or to be more accurate, aluminium foil, can be very useful around the camp kitchen. For those with the space I suggest taking a good healthy supply, but even the backpacker should be able to find room for a more reduced supply. For its weight, few cooking items are so versatile.

### Spoons, spatulas, scrapers and such

Good old-fashioned wooden cook's spoons and spatulas usually accompany us. I wouldn't expect a backpacker to carry these of course, but they make life much easier for the vehicle camper. We prefer wood, as it's quiet in transit. It's also surprisingly light. You could make your own on site of course, and we often add to our collection while camping, but always try to start with one 25cm (ten inch) beech spoon and a spatula.

I'll be leaving the matter of cutlery, plates and the like, what you eat off and with, to you. These are personal choices after all. Any measuring of ingredients out there is unlikely to rely on weights though, and as the recipes given at the end of this book also use them, a teaspoon is likely to be helpful. Alternatively, if you need to keep kit weight and volume down, having a good idea what your regular eating spoon will hold would do. My lightweight stainless spoon, a regular kitchen variety, holds roughly the same as two teaspoons for example.

The 'such' bit in the heading is there to cover all the other sundry items that make cooking in the wild more pleasurable. This can include a tin opener if you carry tins, a roll of paper kitchen towels, a combination plastic sponge/scourer and a bottle of universal biodegradable soap for washing up.

Our French cast-iron pot, doing its thing in Arctic Sweden.

You could make your own of course, but it's probably best to start with something stored already in a pack.

## Mixing bowl

For anyone with concerns about the weight or bulk of their kit, one of the saucepans or a food bowl can be used perfectly successfully to mix food. If space and haulage capacity isn't an issue, a dedicated mixing bowl can be useful, and we often carry a stainless steel version on our canoe camping trips. It's pretty thin, and not nearly as heavy as it might sound.

## Measuring jug

The same comment can be made in the case of a measuring jug. A small plastic one doesn't weigh much, and could even double up as a mug if you wanted to restrict kit expansion. You could of course tackle the measuring jug situation from the other direction, and filled to normal drinking levels, my mug holds half a pint, or about 300ml, for example.

## Baking paper

Baking parchment is certainly not essential, but if you plan to bake anything sticky a piece or two cut from a roll, or a sheet of reusable Teflon tray liner, stuffed down the side of a food container will take up no room at all.

## A grater

While a knife can manage most tasks, a flat grater can be surprisingly useful if you have room and plan to add cheese, creamed coconut or lemon zest to your food.

## Head torch

And finally, before addressing the matter of how to carry everything, a brief mention of head torches. These rather wonderful devices might seem a rather odd item of kit to cite in relation to camp cooking, but a mention will seem very valid as soon as you begin to prepare a meal late on a November afternoon in Scotland. I rarely travel anywhere without one, even in summer.

Using a head torch, and our stainless mixing bowl, on a late autumn evening.

Kit

## Food (and kit) containers

No matter how you choose to travel, every camper needs to give some thought to how best to contain and carry both kit and ingredients. I've already mentioned two key items while discussing matches – dry bags and clip-lock, plastic food boxes. Designed to keep wet food in, the latter are equally good at keeping wet stuff out, whether it's the result of rain or accidental immersion in sea, lake or river. These tough boxes should keep most hungry rodents from helping themselves to your dinner too.

In my opinion, no camper can have too many dry bags. Available in a range of waterproof man-made fabrics and materials, they can be deployed to protect anything from flour and rice, to a whole range of other, non-culinary and damp-shy items. They can then be stowed full inside other less waterproof but more abrasion resistant storage.

For the backpacker, dry bags can be invaluable for storing and, importantly, separating delicate items inside your rucksack, even if it's just a case of one bag for the

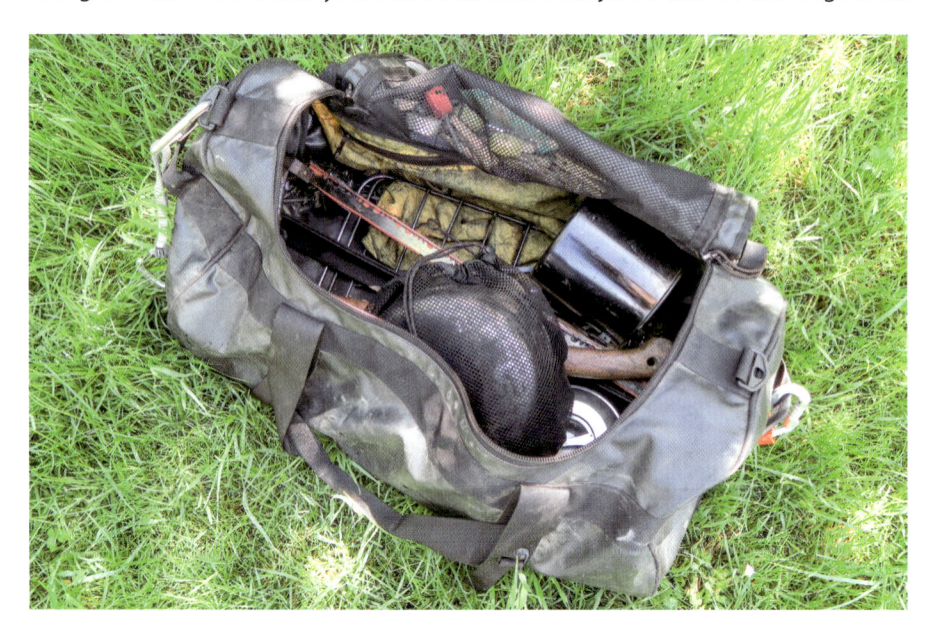

Designed to keep wet food in, and equally good at keeping wet stuff out.

Our kitchen bag, as found when opened. Contents include an axe, bow saw, fire irons, wire grill shelf, a nest of stainless pans, and a billy can. You can also spot a spare fire steel, stored with pegs and other useful odds and ends. Our frying pan would usually be in there too.

46   Kit

ingredients, and another for the cooking kit. The use of different coloured dry bags means that things can also be found very easily. Colour coded dry bag storage cannot be recommended too highly for a camper as far as I'm concerned.

For our van and canoe supported trips, we put our food in a big box. In here, we also store cooking knives, wooden spoons and spatulas, a grater... whatever we'll take to prepare the meals we have in mind.

What we refer to as fire kit – the pots, pans, fire irons, oven shelves, axe and bow saw – live in a heavy-duty zipped holdall. For a long time this has been plastic, but I would rather like to replace this with something in stout canvas.

Our food box is rather more pleasing to look at. Based on the North American canoe food containers, known as wannigans, ours is made from two old wooden wine boxes. More of a wineigan then. It's big enough to carry almost all the food we'll need for a usual canoe camping trip. When not in the canoe, it sits at the very back of our van.

*Our wannigan, or food box, made from a pair of old wine boxes.*

## More unusual cooking kit

### Reflector oven

Armed with just a frying pan and pot, a whole array of boiling, dry-roasting, frying, sautéing and even simple baking techniques can be employed. The addition of some form of wire grill allows... well... grilling. With something like a Dutch oven also thrown into the cooking kit list, although perhaps not literally, true roasting and baking can be added with ease.

Then again, a Dutch oven is hardly portable. In terms of both weight and size, they do require some lugging about. Fine if you have a handy horse or 4x4, but not so convenient if you intend to travel into the wild in a kayak or by motorbike. Even a canoe will struggle a little, if only on safety grounds. Dutch ovens aren't best known for

Kit

their floating qualities after all. If a portage (carry) of any length is likely to form part of any canoe journey, then the last thing you'll want to take with you is a large lump of cast-iron, no matter how keen you might be on bread, cakes or roast venison.

If you are planning to travel light, there's still an option however. A reflector oven can be used to bake and roast. Once the technique has been mastered, and it isn't tricky, it can do the job surprisingly well.

A reflector oven works by capturing the heat from a wood fire in a completely different way to a Dutch oven, or just about any other camp cooking vessel. This adds variety both to the task and the way you can use your fire. The reflector oven is also extremely light, and my favourite version has a trick to make it even more portable. Not only is it much less effort to carry than a Dutch oven, it's probably easier than a lightweight frying pan too.

The principle behind the system is that the oven sits not over the fire, but alongside it, using the metal walls of the largely enclosed space, essentially an open sided box, to capture and retain the radiant heat from the fire, principally the flames themselves. This heat is held all around, even above, the food you are cooking, allowing a surprisingly uniform and even result.

Although specialist reflector ovens are available, a whole array of open-sided metal containers will do the trick, up to a point at least.

Perhaps one of the best known metal boxes that can be pressed into use as a reflector oven, and familiar to anyone who has spent Christmas with Granny, is the one holding the biscuit assortment. Long after the chocolate covered ones have gone, and once that last plain biccie has finally been eaten, these often square boxes can make half-decent reflector ovens. Often the inner tin coating is quite bright and reflective, which helps. If not, lined with foil to increase the heat reflection they are even better. I've even heard of people cooking successfully in reflector ovens made solely from aluminium foil, even folding up the result to be transported and used again. On one occasion, I cooked using a wok propped on its side, and lined with foil, but that propping, and the difficulty in providing a support for the cooking tray inside, meant that this was more fun as a challenge than a sensible way to cook.

Larger, deeper boxes are often better than the biscuit tin, although as with all 'found' versions care should be taken that there are not any visible or even invisible inner coatings or residues that might give off nasty fumes when used. If you have concerns, I suspect a thorough heating before being used should get rid of them, although if you have any doubts then better to be on the safe side and look for something else. I'm also aware that galvanised zinc coatings release a pretty toxic gas when heated (be very careful if you weld it), but have yet to find any convincing guidance on how hot the metal needs to be before that release takes place. I suspect the metal has to actually melt before there's a problem, but as I don't know for sure, I avoid galvanised items altogether.

On a cheerier note, and while these found or emergency boxes will do the trick, there are limits. For a start they are boxes, and they stay that way. Yes, they can double up as containers for other kit during your travels, but once used and sooty, the range of storage options diminishes. Most importantly, nearly all found boxes are also pretty inefficient. Something that is designed for stowage, that can be broken down and packed away, has to be a significant improvement.

The main advantage of a purpose built oven lies in the angled sides. Set at the right slant, these take the radiant heat from the flame, and, as the name of the oven indicates, reflect it back in the exact direction of the food you are cooking. The biscuit tin oven, or anything else with right angled sides, never really puts the reflected heat where it's needed, and in particular, usually fails to apply heat properly to the top of whatever you're cooking.

Those with the right skills and inclination can make pretty impressive angle-sided reflector ovens themselves. I think the model I first used as a Scout had been built by one of the troop leaders. It's quite a while ago now, but I seem to recall it arriving flat-packed, the aluminium sheets having broad tabs that fitted into slots on opposing sides, to be pinned securely in place. If those early campsite memories

A biscuit tin reflector oven, cooking a loaf.

Our Svante Fredén reflector oven, folded for transport – 800g in weight and measuring only 25 x 33 x 1cm.

And in action.

aren't too rose-tinted to be trusted, it worked pretty well. Purpose built reflector ovens that pack flat are a little harder to find. I have spotted a very appealing looking example, made by Pole and Paddle Canoes (poleandpaddle.com), but they are based in Maine, USA.

The reflector oven we use takes the flat pack concept and makes it something of an art form. Svante Fredén has been making his ovens from a shed near Skara in Sweden for decades. He knows what he's doing and one of the trickiest things about using one of his new ovens is the troubling knowledge that you are about to not only get it dirty, but inevitably cover its smart brushed aluminium surfaces with scratches.

I've watched videos of Svante making his ovens. All the work is done by hand, employing an array of manually operated jigs that I suspect he built himself. It is the sequence showing him hand filing the sheet edges smooth that made me appreciate the care he applies to each one. It certainly helped me realise that the reasonably hefty price tag is justified, and that's before I used it.

In terms of portability, the oven couldn't really be bettered. It arrives in an incredibly light thin bundle (800g in weight and measuring only 25 x 33 x 1cm folded). This then displays its great advance on the handmade version I first used, by avoiding any real element of slotting or complicated construction, simply unfolding on neat enclosed pin hinges, to be locked in position by a single rotating tab. And there it is. A stainless steel wire shelf is then slid into place to hold your baking or roasting tray, with another pinned at the back to prop the whole oven at the correct angle for cooking. It looks great.

The Svante Fredén oven isn't particularly big, at least you'd hardly notice it amongst a normal canoe camping load. If you're really keen on the idea it might not even be a problem if carried in a kayak.

Yes, the bread loaves I've produced in the wild haven't been that large, about half the size of the ones I might bake at home, but then that's big enough, and it's pretty easy to just bake another at the next campsite. It also means your bread, real bread of course, is always fresh. It comes into its own when adding either roast potatoes to a main course, or a baked pudding to follow it up, perhaps packed with blueberries or cloudberries.

I guess if you're travelling as a family or larger group, you would probably need something a little larger, although those puddings would probably feed four. If you do need something a little larger, you could have all the fun of trying your hand at building something yourself. Svante has even been generous enough to provide plans for his ovens online (www.sf-canoe.se). I'm sure they could be scaled up pretty easily and put to good use by someone with the appropriate skills.

## Dutch oven

Definitely not for the backpacker, and even a canoe camper will need to think long and hard about this piece of kit. Then again, a Dutch oven is very versatile, allowing you to cook in almost any style you might choose at home – with practice.

Dozens of different companies produce these ovens, sometimes surprisingly cheaply considering all that metal. Look for models with a good lid seal, to keep moisture in and ash out. Another almost essential feature of the cast iron lid is an inbuilt raised lip around the edge, which is needed to hold embers in place for good even baking and roasting. Petromax, the German company famed for their paraffin pressure lamps, make some lovely Dutch ovens in a range of sizes.

If you are going to go for one of these ovens, a good length of stoutish chain and a couple of heavy wire hooks will mean you can use your oven hung from a tripod over the fire. You may, if you have four wheels, even choose to lug a set of steel tripod legs around too.

Purpose built tripods can be bought from a number of companies, including a couple of blacksmiths specialising in bushcraft and outdoor kit. These make life with a Dutch oven very easy, and often look great, but we manage pretty well with

Our Dutch oven, on a road-pin tripod.

The Le Creuset in action.

Using a large Muurikka over a large fire bowl to toast a handful of cashews.

three steel road pins; the sort mentioned above in the fire iron section. Just leant together, so that the inbuilt hooks at the top mesh, and using a pair of stout wire hooks, one at the top, the other at the bottom of a length of chain, the oven can be held easily over the fire at the desired height.

## Cast iron pots

I have to admit that although we own a Dutch oven, and use it occasionally, when we have the carrying power we are much more likely to carry a traditional French enamelled cast-iron pot. Our usual camping pot was made by Le Creuset in the 1970s. This sees a lot of use. The only task a Dutch oven can perform that this pot isn't really suited for is dry baking, and we can employ our reflector oven for that. Roasting inside our Le Creuset works really well, and casseroles... well, that's what they were made for.

We haven't taken it backpacking.

## Fire bowls, griddle bowls or Muurikka

As a very general rule we've found that unless you have a particular preference for a small Muurikka, and carrying and storage capacity aside, the larger bowls are much more versatile. With a dish close to 75cm (29½ inches) across, the full cooking potential provided by the graded temperature range across the bowl, and all that the warm storage space at the edges, can be brought to the fore. Of course other companies produce these very versatile cooking vessels, and we've used griddle pans in a range of sizes made by the German company Petromax.

## Cooking ranges

Although I have seen these in use on many occasions, the last time right up close when the result was a plateful of very tasty grilled salmon, I've rarely cooked with them myself.

Kit

A campfire cooking range, in all its rather medieval glory, cooking salmon (on the board) and baked vegetables (in the foil). Not surprisingly, this range arrived in a van.

Often built by specialist bushcraft blacksmiths, with various methods to hold the fire, your cooking vessels and bare food, involving cantilever arms, hooks and even revolving bits; some are pretty basic, while others look like some sort of medieval siege engine. You really will need something pretty big, with at least four wheels, to carry this to your campsite. This certainly isn't the camp cooking setup for a canoeist, but once in place alongside your Land Rover, Russian Unimog or canal narrow boat, these extraordinary pieces of kit allow for amazing campfire cooking flexibility. These Aga ranges of the outdoor world also hold the fire up off the ground, meaning that not only is there little chance of localised environmental damage, but that you can also cook over wood where uncontained fires are prohibited.

This is our dehydrator.

# Behind the scenes

I've mentioned choices, and I've also admitted that much of what is offered in this book will inevitably represent the methods, techniques and kit we use ourselves. I hope that after a fair few decades of trial and error, at least a few of our conclusions are worth something. One of our most impressive pieces of camping equipment never even leaves home though. This kit item is really useful for any form of camping, whether by van or canoe, but its status is elevated from useful to near essential when it comes to backpacking. This is our dehydrator.

Made in California by the company Excalibur, this is big and pretty expensive, but what it can do has transformed our camping exploits on foot. Anyone who has carried their home on their back for any distance will tell you how important each ounce or gram can be. Carry a tent very far, along with the sleeping bag and all the other items needed to live comfortably out there, and you will soon understand why people cut the handles off their toothbrushes, for example. Of course one of the heaviest items in the rucksack can be food. Delve a little further into the subject and it soon becomes clear that in the makeup of almost any food item, water is the heaviest part. Take the water out, and everything becomes so much easier.

Admittedly, there are a pretty large number of companies out there removing this water for you. The results, sold in cheerfully coloured plastic bags, almost completely covered in lists of ingredients and nutritional information, provide all sorts of meals, both savoury and sweet. They weigh next to nothing. Once water is added, and the whole lot is warmed up, the results can range from really quite tasty to utterly inedible.

What is pretty certain is that these bags will be pretty expensive, at least for the amount you get to eat. In my experience what many dehydrated meal manufacturers judge to be a wholesome meal for a backpacker tends to look more like a snack to me (yes, I may be greedy, but then I only weigh about 11 stone). In brief, the contents rarely look particularly sustaining, even after that water is returned to the mix.

You also have no control over the ingredients. The packet may provide information about even the tiniest addition to your meal, but you can't do anything about it. Even the most unenhanced concoctions tend to have something in the mix I could do without.

And so to our Excalibur.

Through experiment, and within reason, we've found that almost any food can be run successfully through its fan-assisted system. We're always a bit wary of dishes that include meat, as some of our self-sealed meals can sit around for quite a while before being used, but all manner of soups, stews, and other once damp things have been slipped, free of moisture into a well-sealed plastic bag. Once in camp, all that's needed is a billy can, some water and a few flames.

# Kit lists

While many kit items, such as matches, will hold the same importance to the campfire cook, however you plan to set off into the wild, others are obviously better suited to certain forms of transport. This is most evident of course when choosing how to hold your pots and pan over the fire. The backpacker for example is likely to stick either to a tripod or campfire crane, probably built afresh at each stop, possibly backed up by a light folding trivet. On the other hand, the vehicle traveller is probably better off with fire irons, even a fire bowl or Muurikka. When it comes to pots, the walker may manage with just a single billy can, and a lightweight one at that, while the camper using a 4x4 may see a Dutch oven as essential.

Just to ensure that none of the basics are overlooked, and to provide a something of a core kit collection to which other items may be added, here are three lists. The first is designed for the backpacker or cyclist. Inevitably, it's the simplest. The second list adds a few items for a camper using a kayak, while the third offers a basic cooking and fire management complement for the canoeist or van driver.

## Basic kit list for the backpacker and cyclist

The following is a simple kit list, or checklist if you like, for the backpacking or cycling wood-fired camp cook. This catalogue doesn't include personal eating kit such as a spoon or mug. What I consider essential items are marked with an asterisk. The rest is recommended. Any additions should be considered with care – they will all weigh three times as much by the end of each day on the trail.

- Matches* (and a waterproof dry-bag or other container* for protection from damp), stored in the clothes you are wearing

- Spare matches* (with their own protection*), stored in your rucksack

- Modern fire-steel set (so nearly deserves an asterisk of its own, but up to you)

- Billy can (small and light)*

- Kettle (small and light)

- Lightweight chain and wire hooks (* if you intend to use a tripod)

- Cord, or stout string (* if you intend to use the camp crane or tripod)

- Lightweight folding trivet or wire oven grill pan shelf

- Small stove, preferably folding

- Knife*

- Folding pruning saw

- Washing up liquid or soap* – preferably biodegradable

If you really don't like using your hands to break sticks, consider a pair of light secateurs. For those carrying food in tins, a can-opener will be vital of course. If you choose a Swiss-army knife as your cutting implement, this will not only provide this occasionally vital tool, but a whole host of other very useful blades and implements too.

**Basic kit list for the kayaker**

This list is pretty much identical to the one for the backpacker or cyclist, but with a couple of additions, and a couple more asterisks. I've decided to suggest fire irons for those who might choose these as their sole pot support system.

- Matches* (and a waterproof dry-bag or other container* for protection from damp), stored in the clothes you are wearing

- Spare matches* (with their own protection*), stored in your rucksack

- Modern fire-steel set (so nearly deserves an asterisk of its own, but up to you)

- At least one light saucepan with a lid and a small frying pan, or a nest of lightweight pans*

- Kettle*

- Either fire irons, an oven shelf, folding stove or folding trivet*

- Cooking knife*

- Small plastic chopping board

- Folding pruning saw*

- Washing up liquid or soap* – preferably biodegradable

The final paragraph for the backpacker is still just as relevant here.

## Basic kit list for the vehicle supported camper

The following is a catalogue intended for those either travelling by boat or truck, or accompanied by a pack animal; in short, someone who doesn't have to carry the load themselves. You can, of course, add to this collection from items mentioned in the discussions above, depending on the size and oomph of your support vehicle.

- Matches* (and a waterproof dry-bag or other container* for protection from damp), stored in the clothes you are wearing

- Spare matches* (with their own protection*), stored in a kit bag

- More matches

- Modern fire-steel set*

- Frying pan*

- At least one light saucepan with lid*

- Kettle*

- Fire irons*

- Chain and wire hooks (* if you intend to use a tripod)

- Cord, or stout string (* if you intend to use the camp crane or tripod)

- Cooking knife*

- Spare knife*

- Plastic chopping board

- Folding pruning saw*

- Washing up liquid or soap* – preferably biodegradable

- Bow saw

- Axe

A shower of sparks from a modern fire steel, about to ignite a scraped birch bark nest.

# Fuel

When it comes to the question of what to burn, the obvious answer is wood... but, as you've probably guessed, it isn't quite as simple as that.

Then again, before this starts to sound in any way off-putting, it's not much more difficult either. Despite the many lists you might find online citing the fuel efficiency and calorific output of a whole host of tree and shrub species, just about any wood will burn well enough on a campfire, providing anything from a reasonable to excellent fuel – so long as it's dry.

It's true that some woods dropped on a fire, such as spruce or horse chestnut, will spit quite a bit in their enthusiasm to burn, while branches from other species, and I'm thinking here of willow or poplar for example, veer the other way, tending to be right little so-and-sos to get going, before burning ever so reluctantly in a dull sort of way. Mixed with other woods, though, as usually tends to happen on a campfire, they do their bit.

There are also some woods such as laburnum and elder that give off poisonous fumes. This inevitably sounds rather troubling, but then how often are you likely to come across laburnum in the wild. Even the cyanide in elder, scary as that word sounds, is present at such low levels it's only ever likely to cause a problem if burned over an unventilated open fire indoors (the reason why folklore in so many parts of Europe suggests it's unlucky to bring this wood species into a house). Besides, those odd smelling hollow elder stems aren't likely to appeal much as a fuel anyway, unless you're desperate.

Two piles of good dry firewood, seasoned oak on the right, driftwood from the beach on the left.

In the end, much of the wood likely to be found in a British, European or north American coppice and forest will make perfectly decent fuel, including thorn, hazel, crab-apple, beech, Douglas fir, maple, pear, aspen, rowan, larch, Scots pine, alder. You get the picture. Yes, pound for pound, trees such as oak and ash probably produce the best wood for warmth, and are worth seeking out if you know what to look for, but it's all relative, and besides the sudden burst of heat released by wood such as birch or pine can be just as useful when cooking. Often you need something that burns strong and fast. Even yew, known for its poisonous attributes, makes a fine fuel, so long as you don't lick it.

While there can be great pleasure and satisfaction, as well as many practical benefits, in learning to recognise different wood types, and becoming familiar with their various qualities as a fuel, the aspiring wood-burning camp cook really doesn't need to worry too much. Yes, it will undoubtedly help to gain specific knowledge in this area, but an absence isn't going to stop you making a start, and getting along perfectly well too. Almost certainly the best way to learn the difference between, say ash and larch, or birch, chestnut and alder, and to find out what happens when you burn them, is going to come from getting out there and rootling around in the woods, splitting the results and adding them to your fire. Besides, there is no such thing as bad wood, just some species that might be less suited than others. The worst you will end up with is a reluctant fire, and a bit of experimentation with what's available in the locality will probably soon sort that out.

Assuming that it's dry of course. For this reason alone, living wood makes a very poor fuel. As a result, any tree or shrub that's still growing should be left exactly where it is. Not only is felling or cutting branches from a living tree no less than vandalism, live wood, or green wood as it's often called, doesn't burn well at all. No camp meal, unless you really are in dire straits, is worth killing a tree in order to eat it hot. Especially when it's usually so easy to collect something that's dead anyway.

The perfect find; dead, fallen and dry.

You don't even need to find a dead tree to collect enough fuel to cook a meal or two. Despite having cooked hundreds of meals in the wild, I've probably only ever felled a handful of standing dead trees, and even these only in heavily forested locations in northern Scandinavia, where the impact is miniscule. You simply don't need to chop anything down in most situations.

Even the healthiest of trees will shed twigs and small branches in bad weather, occasionally a few quite big ones. Most will also suffer from at least some level of disease, resulting in the dropping of a limb or two. Look under almost any tree and you will find excellent fuel, ranging in size from tiny twigs to whole branches. You just have to pick them up or haul them back to your camp.

The best windfall fuel, as this natural discard is called, will be held up off the ground, where it's kept free from the damp and decay forming bacteria that lurk in the soil. As many branches have sections angled off in all directions, looking like bushy little trees in miniature, only a small portion is likely to be in contact with the ground. The rest will be held high, dry and ready for your cooking exploits. Look up in your search too. Often the best fuel will hang, caught up in the living branches, either within easy reach, or where a well thrown stone or log can soon dislodge it.

Fuel   63

You can see the dark fungal growths in this birch, and it is quite rotten, but it's dry and will make decent fuel for cooking. It'll just burn through faster than sound wood.

Don't worry too much if some of the wood you find on the ground is a little soft and rotten. So long as it's dry, it will still burn, just rather more quickly than more solid fare, producing less heat. Most of our meals are cooked over a mix of solid and slightly rotten wood. Many have been heated using only rather soft, semi-rotten, even quite badly rotten, wood. We just had to stoke rather more often to reach the desired temperature, and you don't build a bed of embers so easily. One of the other slightly positive things about rotten wood, if it is damp, is that being fairly porous, it will often dry through pretty soon if stacked close to the warmth of your blaze.

So how can you be sure your twig, branch or even tree is really dead? Well the first and most obvious clue, at least in the warmer months, is a lack of leaves. If these are present, unless very brown and shrivelled, then it has been off the tree for too short a time. The next test, and the one you'll need to employ in the leaf free winter months, is simply to try breaking a thin section. If your selected piece cracks with a good clean snap, then carry it in confidence to your fire. If it bends, or breaks leaving a section hinged between the two parts, it's still green, and is best dropped.

Where you are faced with what looks to be a dead tree, and you feel that felling it is justified and not too detrimental to the woodland (and remember, a lot of things such as beetles, and even birds, like to live in dead trees), try the lick test. This involves taking a knife or sharp axe (of course it's sharp), slicing away a small patch of bark and cutting a little into the underlying wood. Then lick the exposed bare patch. If it feels warm and dry, sucking the damp from your tongue, even sometimes causing the two to stick together gently, then the wood is almost certainly dead, and has been long enough to produce some decent fuel. Wood that is unpleasantly cool and slimy will stay that way if it's cut up and dropped on your fire. All things considered, I suspect it's probably best to make this test when nobody is watching.

The other almost totally reliable source of firewood, even when no trees are present nearby, is the water's edge. Beaches can be very generous, and Susannah and I have cooked countless meals with no more than the pickings from the shore of a lake or the sea. I recall one particular lake edge in Arctic Sweden, where the sun-bleached timber was so thick on the ground we managed to cook for two days without ever leaving camp. For the first day I had only to lean to one side to grab another clean dry branch.

It's true that the salt in wood found by the ocean, while producing some surprisingly pretty coloured flames, is probably not that good to breath in, but knowing that and avoiding the smoke, I suspect you'll be just fine. Flotsam gleaned from the edge of a freshwater lake is perfectly okay of course, or nearly all of it. Care should be taken both here and at the tidal edge to avoid painted timber, and also to be aware that some preservative treatments aren't always that easy to spot on a weathered piece.

The other fuel source you will come across occasionally in the wild is a tidy pile of air-dried logs, stacked to one side of a well-used fire pit. Sometimes these even hide dry beneath a sheet of birch bark or carefully overlapped planks. On meeting such generous thought and consideration (we've even found matches hidden amongst the pile before now, and on one occasion an axe) I always endeavour to leave that campsite as I found it, or very nearly anyway. Often I attempt to make my replacement pile just that little bit larger than the one we found.

Beaches can be very generous.

A mix of hard and soft woods, with the tools used to produce it. This is the sort of modest log size I prefer to cook with.

# How to prepare your wood

Whether using a fire in camp to cook or just to keep warm, there really is no need to burn large pieces of wood. For cooking, a much more efficient heat, and far more control over it, can be had with twigs, small branches and thin split logs anyway. Most firewood for cooking needn't be much more than a couple of centimetres (an inch or so) in diameter. Slightly larger pieces are best employed only to build up embers or slow down the rate of stoking. For the main cooking fuel, little preparation is usually required beyond snapping it to a usable length by hand. Remember my recent tool-free wood fire experience in northern Scandinavia. Three weeks of cooking is quite a while, and made possible because of the small scale of the fuel we use.

A key advantage of small cut fuel is that it helps to keep the temperature of a cooking fire even. Large logs, and for cooking that's anything over about 5cm (2 inches) thick, will have a tendency to smother and deaden the heat, even if only for a short while. This will be particularly pronounced if you add two or three pieces at one time to the sort of small fire I prefer to cook over. Then, a few minutes later, as the fire takes hold again and they begin to burn properly, large logs will raise that heat significantly. I will also go on to advocate the use of a fire that is not much bigger than the base of the pan or pot you are cooking in. As the largest is unlikely to exceed about 30cm (12 inches) in diameter, with many pots only 20–23cm (8–9 inches) across, this is the sort of length you'll need.

It should be pretty obvious that cooking over a small fire, burning broken twigs, modest branches and thinly split logs, is also going to result in a much more efficient use of the available wood resource. Each to their own of course, but I often marvel at the amount of timber burnt by some campers when cooking. Yes, there might seem to be a lot of it about, and the stuff does keep growing of course, but then it doesn't take much demand from wood burning campers to make a serious dent in the local supply, especially in areas where this style of cooking is gaining in popularity. Endeavouring to limit the amount of wood used, even when only burning dead windfall, is all important in terms of keeping any impact on the local environment to an absolute minimum. Used with care, I suspect Susannah and I often cook a whole meal, probably including a pudding, while using less wood than many campers burn to boil a kettle for tea.

**Bow saw use**

Of course, there comes a time when the only wood you can find is too big to break by hand, even across your knee. This is when the saw comes into its own. Using a saw is certainly the safest way to reduce heftier timber to a convenient length.

Mind you, even bow saws have an irritating and sometimes painful tendency to jump about, particularly in the early stages of a cut. Deep in rural Wiltshire, I once took a team of budding conservationists into a remote and rather beautiful old wood. Before heading in I'd devoted about two hours to providing them with a careful introduction to bow-saw use. Despite that course, and once at our work site, I decided to warn everyone just once more about the skittish nature of the blade before we started, reminding them all that we were at least an hour by an old series III Land Rover from the nearest casualty unit – a good hour, as we began to prove only a few moments later. For this reason, a booted foot is often much better than a hand when it comes to holding a branch in place for that bow-saw cut.

A boot is often better than a hand to hold a piece of wood steady when sawing.

A good pile of driftwood, all cut up and ready for use.

Everyone enjoys bow saw work.

Despite this tendency to skip about, especially as you try to set the blade deep and safe within the cut, the bow saw is still a very valuable tool when the timber you've found is too thick to break by hand.

A folding pruning saw can be almost as good, at least as long as the blade is sharp, but then that goes for all cutting tools. I really like having one of these saws stored somewhere amongst my kit. There's no doubt a bow saw, with its much longer blade, is far more versatile, and certainly the better tool for cutting thicker sections of branch. Then again, I'm often surprised by how well a pruning saw will do, particularly when dealing with the size of wood I consider best suited to cooking fires.

Even when you want a slow stoke, and larger log sections help do this, your fuel still shouldn't really be more then 5–8cm (2–3 inches) wide. Only when the fire is being used simply for heat or drying should larger pieces be employed, and logs of no more than 10cm (4 inches) in diameter will be fine.

If the local conditions mean you are restricted to the use of larger pieces, my first suggestion is to expand your search. Usable thin stuff is usually to be found somewhere, with a little graft. Besides, I'm hoping to find a reason to avoid the next step, which does start to get a little serious. If you simply can't find fuel in anything but chunky logs, then you will need to split these first.

Of course I haven't yet mentioned how you should split your wood, and the glib answer is very carefully. Any splitting method relies on a sharp blade, the best tool usually being the axe.

## Splitting with an axe

For those with little or no experience of cutting wood with an axe or saw, I strongly advise you to find someone who has. You may well have to pay for that skill transfer, but if you find a knowledgeable and proficient teacher, the price will be reasonable. Besides, the cost of making a mistake out there, simply because you don't have the skills, can be disproportionately high.

Fuel

If finding tuition isn't possible, start small, and make sure your tools are sharp (I know I'm beginning to go on a bit about this, but believe me, you really are less likely to damage yourself with something that you don't need to force).

Try to avoid being too ambitious, at least to start with. Until you've had plenty of practice, pick branches or tree trunks of no more than about 15cm (6 inches) in diameter; 10cm (4 inches) might be a better limit at first. These can be cut into logs that vary in length. Thinner pieces can be sawn into rods of up to 30cm (12 inches) or so. Broader or knotty timber will sometimes need to be cut quite a bit shorter if the resultant logs are going to split easily. Experience will also teach you pretty soon that some wood types split a lot easier than others. You'll also find that logs from certain trees, and I'm thinking now of seasoned elm here (should you ever find this exotic stuff that is), are nigh on impossible. If you know your timber, ash, with its smooth, greeny-grey bark and very straight grain, is nearly always lovely stuff to take on with an axe, or your knife.

But let's start with that axe.

First things first – you'll need to find a solid splitting platform. A decent stand for your log reduces the splitting effort by removing that energy wasting bounce you'll encounter when striking it on bare ground. A platform also ensures that when the splitting stroke works, or you miss your log, your axe blade hits wood rather than soil, or even worse, stones.

Your splitting platform can be either a broad log used on end, or a longer log, with a sizeable flat surface, laid on its side. Just make sure it's good and stable. To achieve this, you may need to indulge in a little light groundwork where you want to position your log, digging a slight pit here, raising the ground there. Your splitting platform also wants to be placed on the ground at a decent distance from fellow travellers (there's little like a camper with an axe to attract a crowd). Apart from the obvious dangers from swinging lumps of very sharp metal, wood has a tendency to spring about a bit during this work.

Splitting wood with an axe. Note the solid splitting platform, and the fact that the wood is placed on the far side. Using this method, a wayward axe will have more platform to hit.

Fuel  69

Dropping down on one knee to split wood with an axe.

Splitting wood with a hatchet. To reduce the chance of hitting myself, I've dropped to one knee, and placed a long log as a barrier.

I've mentioned the risk of a stray axe swing hitting a stone. Of course worse still is hitting yourself. Fortunately, there are a few ways that you can reduce that nasty possibility. One of the most effective, and I'm almost tempted to underline this bit, is to drop down on one knee. This simple measure should ensure that when the axe-head misses (and it is inevitably when, not if), it has more chance of hitting the ground, or your splitting platform, than hitting you. This is one of the reasons, hinted at in earlier discussions, why an axe with a longer shaft is often safer in the hands of a novice than a short-handled hatchet.

To further reduce the risk of self-harm, a log placed on the ground in front of your knees (see the photo on left) provides at least some form of axe-head resistant and pain reducing barrier.

There are of course a number of ways to split wood with an axe, with methods varying to some extent depending on the size of the wood to be split.

Broader, and hopefully shorter, logs can be stood on end and struck cleanly. Before taking that first swing though, place the log at the point farthest from you on your splitting platform. This should ensure that any wayward stroke hits the platform and not the ground, or worse, something with nerve endings. Some wood types, such as the ash I mentioned, will split more easily than others. With almost all logs, if you can differentiate the thinner end from the broader one, striking this is usually more effective. Quite why attacking a log from the upper or outer end of the donor branch or trunk is better I don't know, but I was taught this as a boy on the farm, and it always seems to work for me.

With your log placed ready on its platform, rather than simply taking aim and going for a hefty swing, you can instead choose to use only as much downward force as is needed to 'stick' the blade in the top. The whole lot can then be lifted, the log attached to the axe-head (see the photo top right) and then brought down again onto your timber splitting surface. With perhaps repeated strikes, the head should force its way into the log, causing it to pop apart. This isn't a method I necessarily recommend as a primary approach, but may well become inevitable anyway, once your axe becomes stuck... and sooner or later it will stick.

Alternatively, you could adopt this axe head sticking method, taking any power and literally turning it on its head. Once the axe is lodged securely in the top of the log, simply turn everything upside down, axe and log. Then swing your axe to strike the splitting platform with the back (poll) of the axe-head (see the photo bottom right). This upside down blow will force the log down onto the upturned axe-head very effectively, again splitting it. A number of strikes may well be needed before it gives in. One drawback to this method is that the log can be quite unwieldy up there above the axe, and for this reason this is a method best applied only to the smaller bits. Watch out for a poorly 'stuck' axe! Any log that's not fully attached may well lose its grip during a good swing... another good reason to avoid attracting observers.

A much more controlled, and therefore preferable, way to deal with thinner branches is to work with the stick held in one hand, the axe in the other. With your non-axe hand, hold the thin log out almost horizontally, away from the body, laying

Lifting the log with the axe.

Turning the axe upside-down.

Fuel   71

Horizontal splitting – only really effective with easy-to-split wood, such as ash.

the far end on the splitting platform. This is made easier if you've cut those thin logs slightly longer than usual. The blade of your axe, with the axe grasped in your other hand, can then be held against the wood at the point where it is to be split. Both are lifted together, before being brought down hard against the platform (see photo on left). This method is a little tricky to master, and only really works well with clean-splitting wood, but it is very controlled and probably represents the safest option where a wood such as that sought-after ash allows. Again, if you can use just enough force to stick the blade into the wood before lifting for a proper swing, everything is quite lot easier to control.

**Splitting with a knife**

In the absence of an axe, and when tackling smaller diameter pieces of wood at least, you can use a knife for splitting. For the backpacker, this is likely to be the only option available anyway. You might choose to carry a small hatchet, but they really do weigh quite a bit. However you arrive in camp, your knife will need to be well made, usually with a full tang, and preferably with a fairly thick blade.

With an easy splitting wood (yes, like ash), especially if there are no knots, logs up to 10cm (4 inches) in diameter may be attempted. This is ambitious though, and you'd almost certainly be better off, at least at the start, with far thinner stuff. Whatever size you try, make sure your knife blade is a good couple of centimetres (or about an inch) longer than the log's diameter. The reason for this should soon become clear.

For knife splitting, you will also need a suitable wood baton, approximately 30cm (12 inches) long and 5–6cm (2–2¼ inches) or so wide. For those in the know, a round length of hazel is pretty much perfect. If you are planning to try to split any wide logs (over 8cm, or 3 inches) it may also be a good idea to cut a triangular wedge from the round piece of hardwood first, using your knife to shape a good smooth surface on both sides.

Again in a half-kneeling position (it's easier and safer), place your narrow log upright on the timber splitting base. Holding the knife horizontally, blade resting on the top of the log, use the baton on the back of the blade to tap/knock the section nearest the handle into the upper end, often splitting it before it's fully embedded.

Should the back of the blade be driven in flush, and the log is still putting up some resistance, knock the blade down further by hitting it with the baton opposite the handle. Hit the blade as close to the log as possible, using pressure from your other hand on the knife handle to counteract the blows. Down goes the blade until the log gives in.

It doesn't always work though, and the knife may need to be worked/dragged/wriggled free. If this proves impossible, use your wooden wedge, which can be driven into the split with the baton. Alternatively, saw carefully through the log just below the point where your knife is stuck (but taking care to miss it of course). The log will usually split as you reach the section under the partial crack.

Splitting wood with a good knife.

Two of my favourite kindling materials, dead silver birch twigs, and split and shaved softwood.

Using a knife to start splitting some rather ropy wood (all that could be found on this beach) for kindling.

# Kindling

We've considered the main fuel for our cooking fire, but in order to create that versatile and efficient heat source, we need to be able to light it. This exciting moment requires two other forms of specialised fuel, tinder and kindling. As a result of the specific tasks each will need to fulfil, both these fuel types are characterised by their small size.

Moving backwards in scale from the broken branches and spit logs of the main fuel source, and before considering tinder, kindling is the material that sits in size terms between the two. In reality, all this distinction is really no more than an artificial divide, the difference merely a sliding scale. Tinder takes the initial match flame, or fire-steel spark, and produces a small blaze strong enough to light our kindling. In turn, our kindling comprises any flammable material thin enough to catch fire easily, but then burn long enough to light the main fuel. At the early stages of a fire's life, that main fuel will be hardly larger or heavier than the kindling anyway. I suppose in the end, the kindling is whatever will be piled over the tinder to start the whole inspiring process.

Almost anything that burns easily can be used as kindling; it just needs to be the right size. This can be wood shavings, very thin twigs, dried cow-parsley stems or bracken. In situations where you have very little wispy stuff, you are going to have to produce your own, cutting it from your split wood supply.

Using a knife, almost any wood can be split down to kindling proportions, and this can be either thin shavings, or (and perhaps not surprising when you consider their intended task), match-sized or just slightly larger sticks. On the whole, softwoods such as larch or pine, with high flammable resin contents, are better in this role than most hardwoods.

Even if you might struggle to tell elm from oak, or ash from maple, with a little practice it shouldn't be long before you can differentiate between these and softwoods. In the end, it pretty much boils down to just that... whether they are hard or soft.

Generally speaking, the softwoods, from coniferous trees, are usually rather faster growing than their deciduous cousins, and the resultant growth rings are usually wider apart. I say usually because in the far north, with very short growing seasons, even the rings on pine, spruce or fir can sit very close together.

If you are forced to use hardwoods for any of your kindling, don't feel too hard done by. You just need to cut the shavings or split pieces that little bit thinner.

One positive exception to the softwood mantra is birch. Not only does the bark from this tree make a highly combustible tinder, but dry birch twigs, and slivers cut from split logs burn freely too. If I'm somewhere wild, in search of material to light a fire, I'll always look first for a birch tree. Once I've peeled away a few thin sheets of loose bark for tinder, I'll then hoover up as much of the dead twigs lying beneath as I can, especially the thin wispy ones at the end of fallen branches.

My final comment concerns what are often called fat woods, fatwood, heart pine, pine knots, lighter knots or occasionally lighter pine. Without going into the detail of its formation, which I don't pretend to fully understand anyway, this excellent fuel is simply wood from pine trees that has become particularly saturated by highly flammable resins. These natural oils and gums tend to collect at the stumps of larger pines, right at the heart of the trunk, or around the base of the many branches. When you do find it, the pine smell as this timber is cut is almost overpowering. Because it is much more resistant to rot, due to all that resin, this wood, found as small hard spikes where each branch sprouted, or as a tough spine through the centre, or in larger lumps near the base, can at times be simply plucked from a fallen tree and lifted away from the rotten material around it. Occasionally you will find a standing pine skeleton made up almost solely of this prize material. The best I ever found was on a small island in a lake near Arjeplog in Sweden, the last remains standing not very tall amidst its offspring. Split or shaved into dark orange flakes, pine fat woods takes a flame immediately, burning hot and bright. If you do come across any, it is worth tucking some away in a bag for those wet, windy fire-lighting days when even the experts have to concentrate. I still have a few Arjeplog slivers at the bottom of my Brady bag.

Pulled from where it's stored carefully in my shoulder bag it doesn't look like much, but shavings taken from this piece of Swedish pine fatwood often make all the difference when trying to light a fire in tricky conditions.

Rich in the oil lanolin, sheep's wool catches fire easily. This is where it can often be found.

In summer or autumn, you could do worse than just a handful of dry grass.

# Tinder

Before moving on to the fire itself, a last few words about one particular fuel type, an important one, the material that's often key to making that blaze possible in the first place – tinder.

With origins in old Germanic languages and in widespread use in slightly varying forms across north-western Europe, the word tinder describes any combustible material able to take an initial fire-steel spark or flame from a match, and turn it into a flame strong enough and long lasting enough to set light to the fire's kindling. If you think about it, that's quite a challenge, requiring a substance that on the one hand will catch fire very easily, yet will burn long enough, and hot enough, to set the kindling around it ablaze. For most modern campers, since the advent of matches and gas lighters, the ability to catch, hold and develop a spark is not so crucial, but a good tinder is still often vital in those early moments in the life of fire.

As long as they are dry, many substances make fine tinders as they stand. These include dead grass and goose grass (*Galium aparine*, also commonly known as cleavers), fallen pine needles, many forms of fungi, bird down, and in the right season at least, the fluffy and often cited fluffy seed heads from old man's beard (*Clematis vitalba*) and bulrush (usually *Typha latifolia*). Even wool, rich in the oil lanolin, will do. This can often be found snagged on a barbed-wire fence. In fact, almost anything dry and combustible can be used as a tinder.

Unless it's already very fine, such as feathers, wool and many seed heads such as rosebay willow herb (*Chamerion angustifolium*), the key to a good tinder lies in reducing it by splitting or shredding until the surface area of the thin slivers is proportionately high in comparison with the overall volume. This allows plenty for the spark or infant flame to latch onto. Good dry wood, particularly resin-rich softwoods, shaved into thin slivers or match-like sticks, will make great tinder. The pine fatwood mentioned above doesn't even need to be cut that thin.

Some campers will advise the production of pre-made tinders using materials such as highly flammable Vaseline, often smeared onto cotton wool. These work perfectly well of course, but I don't think you need them. Besides, I'd rather leave these crude oil-based products well away from of my campfires anyway.

Mind you, keen to stick to nature, campers often fail to appreciate just how effective paper can be. Many of the materials mentioned can be just brilliant when attempting to light a fire with a fire-steel or bow-drill, and this is just fine when the mood takes you. But then I'm hoping you've taken note of my comments in the kit section, and have at least one full box of matches hidden dry in a pocket. With these, and when it's available, a few sheets of almost anything papery can be very handy. It is basically wood pulp after all. Just ensure that each sheet is separated and scrunched up to allow the flame, and it's all important air supply, space to move about and develop freely. Avoid anything glossy though. The constituents used to make paper shiny often include clay, which will inhibit its flammability. Really glossy paper can be surprisingly difficult to light, and the cause of many a frustrating attempt to add flames to a pile of sticks.

By far and away my favourite tinder, and a natural material always to be found in varying quantities in a reindeer skin bag stored in my Brady shoulder bag, is birch bark. This can be collected from any birch tree, even live ones, without harm. Just remove the wispy bits that hang loose, even pulling free the outer layers (but not going in past the layered outer skin). The bark can be used as it is. Filled with various highly combustible natural oils, it will take a flame even when wet. If the inner fibres of the removed sheet are roughed up lightly with a knife blade, producing a little fibrous nest, a spark from a fire-steel will soon catch and produce flames.

Collecting birch bark in Finland.

A good handful of bitch bark, enough to light a fire.

Fuel

A stack of elegant cut logs lies close by.

# How To Use a Wood Fire

So we have our camp kitchen kit selected carefully for the job in hand. A pile of dry firewood, ranging in size from the wispiest of kindling to a stack of elegant split logs, lies close by. All that's needed now is that fire. This chapter deals with lighting our little outdoor cooker and using it safely, effectively and responsibly.

However, before we can deal with the fun part, the bit where we create our little cooking heat source, there are a few serious matters to consider. Because the intrinsic qualities of a fire are not all positive, the list is quite long too. Don't worry though, before long, once we've considered various matters of safety and first aid, we'll reach the bit where we collect together some tinder and kindling, and introduce a flame.

## Where to light a wood fire

Before considering the nuts and bolts of the process, the lighting and maintenance of our fire, we need first to give some thought to location. For various reasons, choosing the right place to light a fire isn't always simple. A number of factors play their part in selecting the best spot, including practicality, efficiency, safety and the law. These decisions are not just restricted to the campsite itself. First we need to consider the wider setting. The sad fact is that all too often we're not actually allowed to light a fire at all. Even where camping is encouraged, cooking over wood may not be permitted.

The sort of thing we just don't want to see out there, and one of the reasons why campfires are so often prohibited. This disgrace was found in a National Park, right at the edge of a nature reserve.

Using our small flue stove in an area of peaty soils, set on a stone.

While it could be argued that these prohibitions are frequently the result of misplaced caution, all too often they represent a reasonable response based on hard-learnt experience. Sadly there are many campers out there who shouldn't be allowed near a lit candle, let alone a lit fire. The result of their ignorance and lack of consideration is a grim litany of oversized and litter-strewn fire pits. Often these eyesores are accompanied by acts of inexcusable damage to the surrounding vegetation. The rest of us suffer as a result. So, whether it's Local Authority byelaws, National Park regulations, or landowners with a collection of often all too justified concerns, we can frequently experience a ban. Before putting a match to your little bundle of dry tinder and kindling, it really is a good idea to make sure that nobody is going to arrive, red-faced, waving a rule book.

Some places, even whole countries such as Finland, only allow fires when they are lit off the ground. This is where one of those large steel fire bowls or Muurikka can save the day for the campfire cook.

On quite a few occasions, setting out with the canoe, and knowing we intended to camp somewhere that really did need to be looked after (but where fires were allowed), we've taken our stainless steel flue stove. On site, this is set up on a flat stone, usually to be found somewhere. Once the meal had been cooked and the fire finished with, the stove was packed away, the ashes dispersed carefully and the stone replaced. You could hardly tell we'd been there.

Then there are those perfectly understandable situations when a temporary ban is put in place. One of these circumstances will be drought, something we can experience even here in Britain every now and again. But then these should be occasions when even the most experienced outdoor type would hesitate before putting a match to kindling (and then probably decide not to anyway). The results of a cooking fire spreading to a tinder-dry woodland understorey just don't bear thinking about, much less experiencing.

Anywhere with the peaty soils prevalent in many upland and moorland settings should also be approached with great care. Peat, which has been used as a fuel in many of these areas for centuries after all, is highly flammable. A fire lit here has the very real potential to ignite the very ground you're standing on.

We once camped on a small Swedish island, set in the middle of a gem of a lake not far below the Arctic Circle. At first we thought nothing much about the relatively clear area. We were just rather pleased to find somewhere free of undergrowth and baby birch trees to pitch our tent. It was only as we started to wander in search of firewood that the damage started to become apparent. Few of the local trees had been spared completely. Aware of the risk in these locations, I'd chosen to light our campfire on a small patch of beach. This area of gravel was tiny, and I even needed to wear wellies to use it properly, but this was much better than the risk of inadvertently lighting the peaty soil of the island again. Judging by the regrowth, the blaze must have occurred some ten or twenty years before, but at least a dozen pine and birch trees had been killed, three or four still standing charred and leafless.

However, before all this begins to sound too disheartening, there are many situations when a small fire, lit to cook, is not only safe but completely appropriate. These fires offer the camper a chance to experience one of the most significant acts in our evolution and development. I for one would be appalled if this opportunity was lost.

A pleasant enough scene, until you look closely and realise only about half the trees are alive. All the others have been killed by fire, almost certainly caused by someone lighting a wood fire directly on the ground and igniting the peaty soil. The rocky shoreline might be slim, but it will do for our little blaze.

The sort of place we'll choose to cook, as far away from avoidable risks as possible.

How To Use a Wood Fire

A shingle beach; and one of our favourite places to cook.

So once you're sure that no prohibition is about to be infringed, and the immediate location is suitable, a good campfire spot needs to balance two seemingly opposing factors. On the one hand, to reduce unnecessary effort, you want your fire to be close to a decent supply of fuel. On the other, you don't want it so close that you run a risk of lighting that too. In fact, any fire that causes the slightest damage to the surrounding vegetation, even short-lived, is a failure. This includes the vegetation above you.

While taking everything into account at eye level, maybe even a little higher, many novice fire builders fail to look up. This is vital in any woodland setting, but even on a beach, where only one or two trees may be growing nearby, branches can extend a remarkably long way beyond the trunk. What's more, please don't think that just because the leaves or twigs seem to hang way up high, that they are safe. Even when the damage isn't immediately obvious, the heat from even a relatively small fire can rise a long way, shrivelling leaves and searing bark, twigs or leaf buds. Wherever possible, especially on a still evening when the heat will rise undissipated, light your fire with open sky above, and preferably with a fair bit clear on all sides as well. If this just isn't possible, light only the smallest fire under branches hanging no closer than about 6m (20 feet).

For all the reasons mentioned, my favourite spots for a fire sit on sand and shingle beaches or banks. In close proximity to water, this is obviously a good move from a safety perspective, but importantly, these surfaces are also fire proof.

**The wind**

One final matter to consider when it comes to fire location will be the wind. All fires need air, or at least oxygen, and a gentle breeze will often be a positive boon to a cooking fire. It doesn't take much of an increase in velocity however, before that blast becomes less helpful. At the very least, a stiff breeze will quite simply blow any heat sideways and away from your pot or pan. Any stronger gusts can threaten the very existence of the fire; I've seen fires literally picked up before now and distributed over the surrounding area. Not a great idea, and often far from safe for nearby camping kit or the local environment.

Often, some form of natural shelter can be found; a dip in the ground or a collection of trees, bushes or boulders. Sometimes though, where the camping site is featureless, or the wind picks up once the fire is lit, you'll have to create your own barrier. Bags, boxes, even your own body or those of fellow campers may have to be employed. Experiment is usually required to hit upon the best protection. Also, keep an eye that combustible things don't get too close, and try to avoid using anything such as food containers, where the contents might suffer from a little warmth.

Often a shelter will actually make things worse, especially if it's the wrong height, or placed too close to the fire. You'll soon know if you haven't got it right. A downdraft caused on the lee side of the wrong box, or a box in the a poor position, can flatten the fire, pushing the heat away from whatever you're trying to cook. In just slightly the wrong place, your barrier is also likely to exhibit a particularly annoying tendency to drive smoke out in all directions. Not pleasant. Even a shelter that's working, deflecting the worst of any wind effectively, will tend to pull smoke back towards itself, and you. Often fiddling with the box, bag, or camper, placing them at just the right angle to the breeze will result in those offending smoky billows being blown away; but not always.

We found this fire pit on an Arctic island, with stone slabs already set upright in place to provide protection from what must be a pretty troublesome wind.

## Keeping pain free (or safety)

Some books offering advice or guidance these days can seem, at least to my eyes, to get rather carried away about safety. The authors seem to forget that most adults possess both a reasonably well-functioning brain and a good dollop of inbuilt self-preservation. After all, if they've managed to live long enough to earn the money to buy a book, the chances are they've picked up a fair amount of applicable experiences along the way too.

But then fires are a little different, especially as fewer people these days are fortunate to grow up in a house heated by them. It may be blindingly obvious that you can burn yourself with a fire, but perhaps not quite so apparent just how easily this can happen, or the grim extent of the results. Seeing someone burnt badly in camp is a great way to reassess the whole fire/risk thing, but not a lesson I'd recommend.

How To Use a Wood Fire

You probably wouldn't think it necessary to have to point out that petrol and fires are far from a good mix either, but then I've witnessed the results of someone giving it a go, and this took place almost immediately following just such a warning. Leading a conservation team, and complying with contractual stipulations, I'd made the unhealthy repercussions of a petrol fire mix quite clear in a morning safety talk. Or at least I thought I had, only to find myself driving one participant to hospital that same afternoon. Thankfully, that particular instant facial makeover wasn't permanent. So there it is – warning given.

The other real life example I've witnessed involved man-made fabrics. You may have heard how easily some artificial materials can catch fire. All I'll say is the warnings are true, and once properly alight, many are also worryingly hard to put out.

At the very least, sparks from fires can ruin a nylon tent or Gore-Tex coat in about as long as it's taken me to write this sentence. Natural fibres, such as wool and cotton, will also burn of course, but are much harder to light, usually smouldering slowly. Wool in particular often provides a pretty good stinky warning before things get out of hand. The only real worry with natural fibres might arise if you've treated your cotton with some form of waterproofing agent, when things could suddenly start to become rather concerning again.

## First aid

As the subject of safety has been raised, now seems as good a time as any to mention first aid. The first, and easy, comment concerns first aid kits, with the simple advice to carry one. It is then only a matter of reiterating the comments in the Kit chapter, urging everyone to make sure it's comprehensive enough to cater for the whole camping party, and preferably one put together to deal with outdoor activities.

And so to the first aid itself, where I'll start by making a clear declaration. While I've received first aid training as many times as some instructors have provided it, I am not qualified in any way to offer any formal comment. However, as there are a number of very obvious risks involved in cooking over a fire, or at least they should be obvious, I think it only sensible to make just a few observations. What is mentioned here is raised tentatively though, with the clear caveat that my advice cannot in any way stand in for, let alone replace, the knowledge to be gained from dedicated and qualified instruction. A first aid course, especially one tailored to deal with outdoor activities, will always be worth the fee.

Now anyone that knows me will be pretty certain that 'Tidy' isn't my middle name. One glance inside my shed will banish any doubts. So you might be surprised if you were to walk into one of our camps. Yes, the neat surroundings may have much to do with Susannah's intrinsic sense of order and cleanliness, but once a tent is up, and a fire lit, I tend to become infused with many of the same tendencies. The reason... experience.

Along with a real distaste for not being able to find things, rests the knowledge that accidents are far less likely to happen when situations are familiar. As the saying goes 'a place for everything, and everything in its place.' For obvious reasons, trips and stumbles close to a fire are never a good thing for, and much of the risk is obviously removed if nothing is left lying about underfoot. I mentioned earlier in this book that each of our campsites follows a familiar theme. This is why. Attempting to replicate the same layout at each site comes not only with the benefit that tools and other items are usually where you expect to find them when needed, but are therefore less likely to catch you unawares.

On the same theme, and without letting it spoil your fun out there, it is worth developing a campsite tendency to give your next move just one more thought before making it. A cut hand at home is irritating; in the wild it could be really inconvenient. Broken bones don't bear thinking about of course. So try to cultivate the habit, before each action, of devoting a brief moment to consider the following sort of questions – What's under my hand if I put it down for support? What's just behind me if I take a step backwards with this axe in my hand? Is that log stable enough to take a pot of freshly boiled water? And the really obvious one – is the handle to that pan still hot?

*It is worth developing a campsite tendency to give your next move one more thought before making it.*

A tidy campsite reduces the risk of many sorts of injury.

With that potentially painful thought to the fore, consider wearing a pair of gloves around a fire. Not all the time of course, which would be hot, and boring, but whenever you're about to handle something around the fire. Some form of hand protection really can make all the difference when shifting pans of hot water, or fiddling with a log that has been in the fire for a while and needs a little shove to push it into a position where it will catch light. A pair of gloves can be a very sensible idea while cutting wood too. It's not just the bow-saw blade that's sharp, and I've suffered quite a few uncomfortable, but thankfully minor, cuts from a section of split wood before now.

Should you receive a burn, what then? Get it into cold water fast. This shouldn't be difficult near a stream or lake, but if you are cooking somewhere slightly barren, it's never a bad idea to have a bucket of chilly wet stuff close to hand – literally. After that it's over to the first aid kit.

For those that haven't heard about this before, it will probably come as a surprise to learn that one of the most sensible things to take into the wild as part of our first aid kit is cling film. In short, this sterile material can provide an extremely effective replacement skin, should you be so unfortunate as to burn your original. It will not only help to keep the damaged area free from infection, but by sealing all those exposed nerve endings, help to reduce any pain.

When I was first introduced to this novel use, the instruction was to ensure the troubled area was thoroughly cool, and then wrap it in the film. Speaking to a paramedic a couple of years ago, I learnt that the latest thinking, or it was latest at the time, was that this could result in problems, should the area swell. As this seems a pretty likely development following a burn, this makes sense, and the advice I was given was to just lay a sheet of cling film over any burnt or blistered area, once completely cooled, holding this in place with no more than a lightly wrapped bandage.

Noting this particular change in approach, I will reiterate that this isn't the place to provide anything more than the briefest comment on first aid methods. Procedures change, and even if you have had some first aid training, a refresher course is rarely a bad idea.

The last word on all this grim stuff considers any situation that grows particularly ugly. Should that burn cover more than a small area, the cut fail to stop bleeding, or you or one of your party manage to do something even more concerning, just make sure you have the means to call for help. Also ensure that you know the phone numbers and distress signals used in the area in which you're camping.

It's a really good idea to make sure you know the emergency phone numbers for the area you're visiting, and not a bad move to store them in your phone before setting out.

# Lighting

Having considered that rather broad array of troubling subjects, we arrive finally at the bit we've all been waiting for; lighting your fire.

Wherever you choose to do this, preparation is needed first. This will make fire management a little easier, and help you leave the area as you found it once your belly's full and you've finished with it. On sand or shingle, start by producing a slight

Left: graded piles of firewood.

Right: a bed for your fire, laid on bare soil.

Birch bark.

depression. This doesn't need to be very deep, just a shallow scoop a touch larger than your anticipated fire. In a woodland setting, any combustible leaves and other vegetable matter will need to be skimmed aside to expose the bare soil, aiming for at least a hand's breadth clear around this slight depression.

Before you do anything with your cleared area, gather plenty of the dry fuel discussed in the last chapter. This should range from the smallest wispiest stuff for tinder, to a few thin branches (remember, only one or two inches in diameter). Cut these into 20–30cm (8–12 inch) sections (depending on the size of your cooking vessel), placing these in piles, or better still, graded piles, on the up-breeze side of your scoop. If you can only find pretty hefty wood, split this down before going any further. These piles of sorted fuel should be placed at arm's length from where you are kneeling – within reach, but safe from accidental combustion.

Then, make a little bed for your baby fire to sit on... seriously.

Using short lengths of dry twig, about 15–20cm (6–8 inches) long, lay a handful close together to form a mat. This very slightly raised platform will help keep your tinder dry, insulate the infant fire from the cold and probably damp ground below, and burn itself to provide a good bed of embers quickly – the principal aim for cooking.

While you can experiment with a host of natural tinders to light a fire, some of which were mentioned at the end of the last chapter, there is really nothing wrong with scrunched-up paper. I've already mentioned my favourite tinder, birch bark. It

Left: a feather stick, cut from spruce.

Right: making a feather stick, using a solid working platform, and keeping everything braced so that the cutting angle remains constant.

really is amazing stuff, filled with extraordinarily flammable natural oils. Just hold a lit match near the thinnest papery edge. You will have fire.

Once you have a handful of tinder resting ready on its mat, cover this with a good bundle of very thin completely dry kindling. Remember, softwoods such as pine, spruce, larch and fir, all contain more combustible oils and resins than the likes of pear, thorn, or wild cherry. Thin shavings cut from these woods are far more likely to catch and hold a new flame than those trimmed from most hardwoods. If only hardwood is available, just cut it thinner.

Many fire-lighting aficionados like to produce what's called a feather stick, basically a thin split section of softwood, or perhaps sweet chestnut if you know your trees, from which numerous long curly shavings are pared, but not quite removed. In skilled hands, starting with a split section of wood up to 30cm (12 inches) in length and probably no more than 3cm (1 inch) thick, it doesn't take long. With not a great deal of practice (and success is all down to maintaining the correct blade angle through the cut), you can shave down from near to the top, reaching almost, but not quite, to the bottom, ending up with something that looks like a small wood spring tree. If you find this quite tricky, turning the stick the other way up, working with the grain of the wood in the other direction, may make all the difference. Once completed, and with all that thin cut wood held in one place, these make great natural firelighters.

Birch bark tinder on the fire bed.

How To Use a Wood Fire

The baby fire, just before bringing in a flame.

Returning to our proto-fire, and with the very smallest stuff at the bottom, build that pile of kindling on your mat. And while building, try to think like a flame. Make sure there's enough room for the flame to move, and the all-important air to get in. At the same time, make sure it's not so loose that the flame has nothing to bite into. Judging this will take a little practice, but before long thinking like a flame will become second nature.

One last comment. Make sure you have at least twice the amount of kindling needed to build that first pile. Held in reserve, this will be required to feed the fire in the crucial early stages as the initial blaze consumes what you've heaped up – we hope.

For the actual lighting flint and steel, fire-lighting bows and other mysteries of the fire-lighting art are all very well, and great fun for the initiated. I'm fairly sure that with experience you'll want to try them, but for now, I suggest that if you want to add some colour to your sausages, just use that box of matches, or a lighter.

Once lit, go slowly. Don't be in a rush to lob on any big stuff. Just add the smallest reserve twiggy kindling bits or softwood slivers gently as the fire starts to take hold. Once you are sure your fire is properly alight, add slightly larger twigs or thicker shavings. And should everything begin to look as if it's dying back, return to the very thinnest stuff for a while. This is why you need to ensure you have a fair amount in that reserve pile. If things start to look worryingly quiet, a small strip of birch bark often does the trick.

At this point you may need to increase the supply of oxygen to your infant fire. This can be achieved in a number of ways, the most common being probably one of the oldest tricks known to man, using your breath. This is one of those activities that seem, at first sight at least, to be quite simple, but also require a definite feel for fire. Go in, all guns blazing, and you're as likely to blow everything out as kick it into life. The trick is to apply just enough artificial breeze to enliven any glowing bits, but no more. Once things are under way again, with a good show of flame, then you can usually blow as hard as you like. Two final comments on this method though: watch out for your eyebrows, hair and or hat, as things can burst into life quite enthusiastically at times; and when you want to take your next breath, be kind to your lungs by simply turning your face away from the fire before inhaling.

A hat, at least one with a good brim, can be employed to provide the air for you, with the same precautions in mind. I've seen more than one baby fire blown right off its little bed before now by an over-enthusiastic waft.

The last trick here is to use the telescopic blowpipe, mentioned in the kit list. These can certainly keep everything clear of the smoke and any flame, but their other benefit lies in the ability to put a concentrated blast of vital air right in deep where it's needed, without having to disturb the fire and possibly snuffing it out, at this vulnerable early stage.

Whatever method you employ, work at it all patiently until you have proper blaze before adding the bigger stuff.

As you add fuel, remember to keep your alter ego as a flame in mind. Try not to add your sticks or split logs in one go, or all dropped in the same place. As each batch goes on, attempt to leave plenty of gaps for the air to get in at the bottom, where your

Getting in there to use lung power to liven up a fire, and a pretty clear example of one of the disadvantages.

A telescopic blowpipe in use to put flames back amidst some reluctant kindling.

How To Use a Wood Fire 91

A good bed of embers.

fire should be burning hottest, and for the flames to reach up and find something new to latch onto. Perhaps the best way to do this is to lay a pair of well-spaced sticks in one direction, adding the next pair at right angles, almost as if you are building a small timber tower. In fact, this is what you will be doing. This should ensure that both essential oxygen and the resultant flames can move freely and do their bit. All you need do is keep adding fuel slowly, enjoying the glowing results of your work.

Sometimes this approach will leave too many gaps between the fuel, and so the required glow will remain stubbornly absent. A good blow at the base should help, but may only result in a burst of heat and light down at the bottom. This is when your young fire will probably benefit from a little shake, designed to shift any fuel that hasn't yet caught fire, settling it down closer to the hot bits at the base. A shake like this takes a little practice, in part to ensure that this settling doesn't result in you squashing the life out of your fire, but also to safeguard against ending up with an unwanted burn. Using a stick to jiggle everything is probably best, but if the fire needs this sort of shake up, it's probably not very hot anyway, and I often just use a gloved hand... very carefully. Besides, using your hand for a very brief (repeat, very brief) shake allows you to feel what's happening. What you really don't want is to squash everything down too far, and literally snuff out the good bits at the bottom – all that's usually required is a modest shake. With a little practice, getting this sometimes helpful shove just right will be easy. As a final comment: even a mature fire can benefit from this sort of jiggle every now and again, just to drop the unburnt fuel closer to the embers, but this time best not use your hand, even in a glove.

With our young fire now crackling away merrily and consuming our twiggy offerings with gusto, now is the time for a little more patience. Before starting to cook it really is important to wait until a good bed of embers has developed. And remember that hardwoods almost always produce a better crop of these important shimmering coals than any wood cut from a coniferous tree, they just take a little longer.

Finally, at the risk of overdoing this comment, keep in mind that in terms of size, your fire never needs to be much larger than the base of your cooking vessel. If you want a pot and a pan on the go at the same time, simply extend the fire in one direction, producing a lozenge shape to sit beneath both.

# Finishing with your wood fire

And when you have finished with your fire?

Make sure all the twiggy stub ends lying around the edge are pushed up onto the embers to burn through completely. This will significantly reduce the work needed to clean up your campsite.

Next morning, or whenever you plan to strike camp, make sure your fire really is out. Poke about in the ashes, pouring a little water on anything that still glows or smokes, then check it again. Only when you are completely certain it's stone cold (use your hand to check for warmth – well you are sure it's out after all), spread the ashy remains thinly around your area (a small warning here – wet ash is particularly caustic). This small amount of ash and charcoal shouldn't be disruptive to most woodland ecosystems, and of course if your fire was a sensible size, there should be very little left anyway.

Scattering ash, a little here, a little there...

Finally, return the ground to its original form, re-filling and levelling your scoop, spreading the dead leaves and vegetation again if in the woods.

The only time I feel tempted to leave any sign of my presence, is at the site of a regularly used fire pit, when I like to leave some cut kindling and fuel in a neat pile alongside. It can be very pleasant to arrive tired at your campsite in the evening to discover just such a present.

Now step back and feel smug in the knowledge that not only have you re-engaged with one of the most important skills of your ancestors, but you've just cooked free of charge, and without releasing any fossil fuel CO2.

What's more, even you can hardly see where you have been.

Perhaps a little carried away with leaving a campsite as we found it, but very satisfying – washing our footprints from the beach.

# Problem solving

Occasionally, you will find yourself trying to light a fire on a very wet site (we will deal with very wet fuel next). Unless you're forced to work in an area where water is actually pooling, something can usually be done.

We've already covered the advantages of laying a small platform of dry twigs on which to build a pile of tinder and kindling, lifting the infant fire away from the cold and damp below. Where the ground is particularly wet, just increase the depth of the bed, also extending the area a little. Start with longer twigs laid tight together, then place another layer at ninety degrees, even perhaps a third set back on the original alignment. By the time your infant fire has burnt its way down thought this lot, gaining heat and maturity as it goes, it should cope with any ground damp.

In some ways, this method is very similar to the upside-down fire. Here, the whole thing is deliberately built upturned, the initial pile of tinder and kindling placed on top of layers of increasingly big logs. This may well do the trick when all else fails, but due to its height and size can be a little tricky to cook over, and might be best employed for heat and general camp cheer.

In really wet areas, and if somewhere dry-ish just can't be found, I try to build either some form of impermeable layer or a raised platform, sometimes a combination of the two.

This is most easily achieved where you can find a few broad flat stones, laying these tight together where you intend to cook, possibly even overlapping. To stop this platform rising too high I will often dig a bit of a flat-bottomed pit first. This also provides a good wodge of soil, silt or gravel that can be spread on top of your crazy paving. This layer only needs to be 2–3cm (an inch or two) deep, when it will protect the underlying stones from heat and discolouration, and any danger of cracking or exploding (be very careful putting stones too near a fire, as permeable ones that take up water, and you'd be surprised how many do, can shatter as that moisture boils).

A low lying and very damp campsite, with broad stones used to provide a raised platform for the fire.

How To Use a Wood Fire 95

Good dry firewood is often found hung up in the lower branches of trees.

If done neatly, you will end up with just a slight raised area. Where no stones can be found, I lay a collection of long logs, about 8cm (three inches) in diameter, in the flat pit, piling the dug material on top, but to a depth of 5–8cm (two to three inches). This should be deep enough to raise your fire above the damp, and stop these logs catching fire (and remember, it is still going to be wet down there).

Of course your problem may be more to do with damp above ground than below. If the weather has been very wet for a while, the woods or beaches providing your fuel are going to be very wet too. Finding dry wood is going to be tough. It may even seem impossible.

It isn't, and at the risk of sounding as if I'm just showing off, I'll mention my own experiences as encouragement. I once ran forestry conservation projects, often coppicing hazel or clearing heavily overgrown footpaths and bridleways. This meant that for nearly two years, summer or winter, in drought or deluge, my working day began by starting a fire to burn brash. I can recommend this as a way to fine-tune those fire-lighting skills. Although on some days, with the rain hammering down, it might have taken as much as an hour to see the flames burn bright, a fire was always lit.

Success in finding dry fuel (or at least dry enough fuel) can be achieved by perseverance, searching through the woods for tiny pockets of protected twigs and bark. Just make sure it's not at all rotten. Rotten dead wood, even only slightly rotten, will have taken up damp. Sound dead wood on the other hand, with an unbroken bark covering, will have kept that damp out. It is often most easily found hung up in the lower branches of trees or bushes.

The trick in these conditions is to start with fuel cut, or rather shaved, as thin as possible. Even when wet, the surface moisture soon evaporates from a very fine cut sliver, letting the infant flame bite into this wispy stuff.

The other thing is species recognition. Newly dead silver birch will usually burn well. Birch bark, especially the wispy bits lifting off the trunk will almost always catch light even when wet. Despite having witnessed it many times, I'm still rather amazed when I shake the rain off a square of birch bark, touch it with the flame from a sheltered match, to see it catch, crackle and almost boil across the papery sheet. Of course, all this is also made so much easier if you ensure you carry at least a small supply of dry tinder in the first place.

For the fuel itself, the same dead, but sound and not yet rotten, timber is the quarry, only in larger sections. As even this solid wood may have taken up some damp at the edges, the aim is to reach what should be the drier stuff inside. To do this, you will need to split it. So, after finding a good sized dead branch, use a saw to cut a heavier section into logs, and then use an axe or knife to split these, ultimately reaching the dry material at the centre. Try to cut it down small too, as a weak fire can catch onto a small piece of split wood, or at least a bundle of small bits, much more effectively.

My final suggestion is to head out into a damp wood before you go camping, on a day when the chance of a hot lunch or dinner doesn't hang on your fire-lighting ability, and just give it a go. With the pressure to succeed taken off, you may find that lighting a fire in these conditions is not that difficult after all. When you are looking to start a healthy fire on a camping day, it's likely to be a lot easier when you already know it can be done. Confidence tends to breed success.

## Final fireside thoughts

In the introduction, before setting out a few key aims, I listed the things this book was not about. It was not, for example, really about engaging with the past. But note that 'not really'.

Inevitably, from the moment we kneel down beside a small pile of twigs and wood shavings and encourage them to produce their own flames, we reconnect with the day-to-day normality of our ancestors. Our attachment to fire goes back a very long way indeed.

Why not set out to string your first jewel.

That deep connection with a humble campfire should hardly come as a surprise. Apart from being perhaps the oldest thing of beauty controlled by man, it was, for an extremely long time, of immense practical importance. Even without considering cooking, a fire at the centre of group of shelters or huts provided light, warmth, a deterrent to predators and a means to fire pots, harden wooden points, melt resins, gums and resultant glues and sterilise water, to say nothing of its ritual potential, or even its simple aesthetic capacity to please and comfort.

When we set out to cook over a wood fire we do so much more than add warmth to our food, or help release nutrients from raw ingredients. As the flames lift from a shimmering bed of embers to envelope the base of a pot or wrap about the flank of a fish, we shift away from a modern dependence on a sanitised and disconnected energy release, from the suspect consumption of an irreplaceable fuel resource. What we accomplish instead, while employing something truly sustainable (and

I hesitate to use this now debased word), is not just a reforged link with our forebears, but a chance to connect with the intense and enduring beauty of a simple wood fire. It can be deeply satisfying.

Sigurd Olson, the American environmentalist, teacher, writer and wilderness guide was convinced. He often wrote with evident passion about campfires, and once likened the memory of each to a string of pearls. Like the fires themselves, these memories could be blown upon to bring each wilderness night back to life.

I'm not so sure about the pearls. Considering those little conflagrations, I can't help feeling that amber would fit the role better. Whatever the image used to picture these rekindled fires, I can't help feeling this analogy is wonderfully apt. Each campfire is a gem, some prettier than others, some due to circumstances more valuable, but each provides a treasured memory worth salting away for leaner days ahead.

You've read the chapter. Why not set out to collect a little dry wood and string your first jewel.

Two people cooking, one looking after the food, the other the fire.

100  How To Cook Using a Wood Fire

# How To Cook Using a Wood Fire

Once ingredients have been chosen and prepared, cooking success is pretty much all about heat control. Yet while twisting a knob on a gas stove does seem very simple, adjusting heat when using a fire can be as easy as sliding a pot from one side of the blaze to another – really. Other than that single movement, or variations on it, the only other aspect of temperature control to consider is keeping the fire fed appropriately. Before concerns set in, this can be regulated with as little trouble as varying the frequency you add fresh fuel.

With this pair of interlinked tasks, it's here I'll suggest that wood fire cooking is often made a lot easier with two people. Where a brace of campers share the experience, one outdoor chef can focus on the cooking (sliding that pan to and fro, and keeping an eye on what's in it), while the other tends the fire (adding the occasional stick). Using a fire to cook may seem fraught with difficulty, but the whole thing really is very quick and easy to pick up. This isn't to say that you need two people, and I've often cooked quite happily over a fire when alone, as have many others, but it does simplify things, especially at the learning stage.

Going back to that temperature control bit again – as it is key to the whole process – we're going to start by assuming you have your fire going properly. Until sure of this important detail, you'll just be making hard work for yourself. All this cooking over burning wood might be simple, but if it's also a new experience, there'll be enough to think about without struggling unnecessarily to keep a hesitant fire alive too.

Scandinavian kitchen design.

A bed of burning coals will represent the heart of your cooking fire.

It's a lot easier to concentrate on the cooking with a good pile of wood ready to use.

The first thing to do then, once your fire is properly lit, is to let it be for a while. Leave at least ten or fifteen minutes during which you do nothing but stoke gently as the fuel burns through. This very important pause is needed to let your fire bed in.

What we are after, before any cooking takes place, is the development of a good layer of glowing embers. This bed of burning coals will represent the heart of your cooking fire. These ember beds can be used either on their own, when a low even heat is needed, say for grilling or the simmering of a stew, or to provide quick ignition to any new fuel when a burst of increased heat is required. The longer a wood fire burns, the deeper and more enduring that bed of embers will become and the more even the temperature will be.

If nothing else, the ground below your fire will probably be cold. It's also likely to be quite damp, possibly very damp. It can therefore take quite a while for your fire to warm things through and dry them out properly, and both will be needed before your fuel is able to burn efficiently. If we have the time, Susannah and I will let a fire mature for as much as half an hour or more before bringing in a pot.

My other assumption is that you have a good supply of dry firewood cut, ready to hand, nearby. Life around a campfire, at least a life that includes a good meal, really is made so much easier if you can concentrate on the fire, and not its fuel needs. Yes, once experienced, and if operating in some helpful wood-filled environment, you probably can manage both the stoking and the gathering of fresh fuel at the same time, but you're really only making life unnecessarily difficult for yourself when starting out. Remember, you're soon going to be engaged in that all important cooking too. Much better, before making any start, to have built a good pile of fuel, or even a couple of piles, ready sorted, chopped and split.

So, the fire is lit, and there you are basking in the warmth of those glowing embers, a generous heap of assorted sticks and logs stacked nearby. Now to turn a campfire into a cooking campfire, and bring in a pan.

# Pot and pan supports

For many campers, this is where producing a meal over a wood fire can suddenly begin to look rather worrying. The whole thing is so very different from what you're probably used to after all. Cook in a kitchen, and there will be somewhere stable and flat to place your frying pan or casserole pot. Now, crouched by your fire, you're faced instead by flames dancing over a tumble of sticks, split logs and glowing embers. Not on the face of it a very friendly place to try to rest your cooking utensil. What's needed at this point is something to hold your filled saucepan or billycan safely in place. Fortunately, mankind first put their collective minds to this problem many centuries ago. This means there are simply dozens of ways to approach the problem successfully. We'll focus on just a few of them.

It's a slight over-simplification, but campfire cooking has evolved to provide us with pan support systems that can be divided into two general camps (I think there's a pun there); those that support the cooking vessel from below, and those that suspend the pot over the fire from above. In the first group we have fire irons, trivets, oven shelves and camp ranges; in the second, such devices as tripods and various forms of cranes and frames, often constructed from wooden poles.

In addition to suspended cooking vessels, we then have a collection of detached setups, in which the cooking takes place in a freestanding unit. The reflector oven and variations on the Finnish Muurikka fall into this category, but it also includes the versatile Dutch oven, which can be used either on its own, or propped or suspended using a number of the systems just listed.

It has to be admitted that the methods described below make our preferences pretty clear. That's deliberate. Why suggest an arrangement we're not completely happy with after all. Mind you, even this selection isn't that cut and dried. As already mentioned, what may suit a camper heading into the wild in a large truck or even a large canoe, just isn't going to be viable for a cyclist, let alone the backpacker. So the options are not only discussed from the perspective of their cooking merits, but also their suitability to the way you might wish to travel.

Our fire irons, propped on a pair of stones.

A small kettle and a large pan, both supported securely on fire irons at the same time. Just push the irons closer together at one end.

Looking at the systems that support a pot or pan, we'll begin with that first group, the structures that hold our cooking vessel from below.

## Fire irons

As Susannah and I are so keen on them, and they therefore feature fairly prominently in both the kit list and photos, I'm going start this fascinating subject by picturing you setting that pan down on a pair of fire irons.

Fire irons have many advantages. Not least, they can provide a cooking setting that's likely to most closely resemble the one you're used to at home. When I mention sliding a pan from one side of your fire to another to control heat, this is the system I have in mind. Propped side by side on two suitable stones, one to either side of your burning fuel, fire irons provide a very simple yet surprisingly stable support for a wide range of cooking vessels. By adjusting the distance between the two irons – a simple matter of sliding them a little closer together or further apart – anything from a kettle or billycan with a small base, to pretty substantial and hefty cast-iron casseroles can be held, even at the same time. Few truly portable cooking pan support systems are so versatile and reliable. For their weight, none can carry heavy pots with such security.

No more than those two irons need to be carried. The only other requirement is something to support them, and a pair of suitable stones can almost always be found at your chosen campsite. For obvious reasons, two brick-shaped rocks are best, but where only more randomly proportioned lumps of rocks are available, and this is often the case, a hollow can usually be dug in the ground to either side of your fire to provide a stable setting for each stone. In situations in which only a single stone with a broad flat surface can be found, it is still possible to prop the irons. These just lie wide apart on the flat stone, with the other ends tight together on whatever else you can find. The choice of pan sizes will just be restricted slightly by the arrangement.

All is not lost even in situations where no stones can be located. In fact, a pair of logs, about 30cm (1 foot) or so in length, cut from a section of green wood will usually hold out against combustion for long enough to cook a meal, and often provide a more stable setting than any stone. Once the cooking is done, and the fire irons lifted, these often partially charred logs can simply be added to the bed of embers for a little slow burning post-meal warmth.

Whatever support you choose, aim to place the fire irons about 12–15 cm (5–6 inches) above ground level. This will leave room for your fire (remember, I have advised that only thin split wood or sticks are required), while also allowing the base of your pots to sit close to the heat. Adjustments can always be made during the cooking process by simply substituting the supporting stones or logs with taller or shorter versions. Alternatively, you could sink what you have in slight hollows, or mound up a little soil, sand or gravel if you need to lift them. Sometimes, when I need to raise the irons only slightly, I just slip a stick or thin section of split log under the irons on top of one or both of the supporting stones.

***Advantages:*** Simple. Robust. Can carry heavy pots. Can carry pots of differing sizes at the same time.

***Disadvantages:*** The irons are a probably too heavy for backpacking use.

## Oven shelves

A wire shelf from a household oven or grill can also make a very useful support for camping pots and pans. Being pretty lightweight they can usually be carried without trouble by a backpacker, cyclist or kayaker. For those keen to keep weight as far down as possible, some fairly skimpy versions can often be found in the oven grill pan. Most these days are chromed, and therefore easy to clean.

Propped on suitable stone, about 12–15cm (5–6 inches) off the ground, this will give room for a fire underneath, while still keeping the pot base close to the heat. Three stones will always provide a more stable setting than four. Beware though. Unlike

Fire irons propped on a pair of damp lakeside logs.

An oven shelf supporting a pan.

How To Cook Using a Wood Fire

*A small oven shelf, propped on stones, and supporting three pans.*

the fire irons, which tend to stay put, chromed oven shelves are rather slippery, and therefore have a slightly inconvenient penchant for sliding about. It is worth ensuring therefore that the whole setup is as steady as possible before adding a cooking pot. For this reason, pointy supporting stones, wedged a little between the wires of the shelf, are often better than flatter ones.

While rarely very big, an average oven shelf is often large enough to provide room for three smallish pans. If you really do like this system, and have the space and carrying capacity to cope, some really quite substantial shelves lurk in some of the more upmarket ranges.

Wire oven shelves can also be used in conjunction with fire irons and trivets (see below) to provide the perfect grilling surface. I often slide one over our irons to cook fish.

***Advantages:*** Simple. Robust. Often very light. Can carry more than one pot at a time, and pots of differing sizes.

***Disadvantages:*** If chosen for their light weight, often not very big (but still usually large enough for two modest pots). Without care, sometimes a little unstable.

## Trivet

While still on the subject of camping kit that hold pots and pans from below, these little devices combine a flat pot supporting surface and the legs in one simple package. Trivets are very useful items of kit for the backpacker, the best being light and fully collapsible, although they are obviously limited to one pan or pot.

They can though support a frying pan. A trivet can of course be teamed up with other supports such as the tripod or cantilever system to allow two or more pots to be employed at once. As with the fire irons, trivets can also be used to support a small wire oven shelf, thus allowing a backpacker to grill.

*A trivet in use, alongside a camp crane.*

How To Cook Using a Wood Fire

Our trivet, made by our daughter Miranda, has pointed legs. This makes this particular model very useful with fires laid on soft ground, when the height of the trivet platform over the fire can be adjusted simply by altering the depth they are pushed in.

***Advantages:*** Simple. Robust. Often pretty light. Can be used to fry. Can be used to grill with a wire oven shelf.

***Disadvantages:*** Can only carry one pot at a time.

## Tripod

In addition to moving it sideways, the other way to control the heat in your pot is to shift the container up or down, closer to or further away from the fire. A tripod, that suspends the cooking vessel from above, allows you to do both. This setup is also great for the backpacker, as the required materials can usually be found easily enough where you choose to stop and camp. Therefore nothing need be carried but a pot or kettle.

A tripod made from three lengths of hazel.

There are different ways to achieve a workable tripod, but when I want to set one up I take three lengths of straight wood, usually hazel, about 180cm (6 foot) long, and lash them together with stout cord (a spare boot lace works well) close to one end. The feet at the other end can then be spayed out to the side of the fire, producing a stable frame, with the apex directly over the heat source.

I then hang a thin wire double-ended hook (I usually make mine from a clothes' hanger) in the lashing. A length of light chain and can then be hung by a link on this wire, with a further wire hook taking the pot at the bottom. By choosing which chain link I catch at the top hook, I can adjust the pot height above the fire by as little as 0.75cm (¼ inch) at a time.

Depending on preference, and availability of materials, you can of course employ other systems to suspend your cooking vessel, including wire from top to bottom,

A bent wire hanger, hooked into the tripod lashing to hold a chain.

How To Cook Using a Wood Fire 107

heat resistant cord or rope, leather, a wooden hook, even woodland climbing plant stems, or combinations of the above. Anything that can manage the weight and temperature will do. It is very simple for example, to cut an arm's length section of round wood, with a natural hook at one end to hang to hold the pot, cutting deep, slightly upwards sloping slots in the stem. These slots can be held either directly at the apex of the tripod by the lashing, or hung on a short piece of wire, as shown in the photo. With more than one slot, the wooden hook can also be hung at different heights above the flame.

Stout poles, if backed up by suitably robust hooks and chains, can support surprisingly heavy cooking vessels, even Dutch ovens. Steel rods can also be employed in these instances, but take the system beyond the remit of most human-powered travel methods.

*Advantages:* Simple. Depending on the supports, can carry heavy pots. Can often be created from materials found on site, and therefore suitable for the backpacker.

*Disadvantages:* Can only hold a single pot or pan. Only really suitable for boiling and general heating.

A wooden pot hanger, held in place by a short section of wire hooked into the tripod lashing.

## Cantilever, or camp crane

The cantilever system, or camp crane, is just as good for the backpacker, allows fine-tuning of the pot's position in both the vertical and horizontal plane, but is perhaps a little trickier to set up. Mind you, if built well it is very simple and convenient to use.

Start by driving a bare unworked length of straight wood (again, hazel excels here) about 120cm (4 foot) long and about 5cm (2 inches) in diameter into the ground about 105cm (3½ feet) from your fire. If you sharpen one end crudely, this will make things much easier. You can use a stone, a length of heavier log or the back (poll) of your axe to hit it in. Now for the slightly tricky bit.

There are different ways to produce the swinging crane section, and it can even be achieved with one length of wood, but most people select two, and this is the method I find easiest.

Find two more lengths of hazel, or similar, 2.5cm (1 inch) or so in diameter, each with a fork producing two branches. Cut one 75cm (2½ foot) length so that the fork sits at one end of a length, with each divided branch cut down to about 10cm (4 inches). The other is cut, just below the fork, to about 120cm (4 feet) in length, with only one side limb shortened to 10cm (4 inches). These two pieces are then lashed together, and the accompanying photo is probably going to be more informative than any description. A simple notch, cut at the end of the horizontal arm, will help keep any pot chain or wire in place. The photo to the right is best left to speak for itself, and it can be seen that the arm's own weight, along with the weight of the pot, is all that's needed to hold everything in place. Both pot height and lateral position over the fire can now be adjusted with ease.

Of course there is a drawback to any tripod or cantilever system While both setups are great for boiling and simple heating, there is no easy way to fry or grill without specialist hanging equipment. You can devise a system that hangs these grills or wide pans from a single line (or chain) of course, but it all gets a bit cumbersome, and isn't really what a backpacker would choose to carry anyway.

It is here, for the backpacking cook, that I will once again advocate the combined use of a lightweight folding trivet and pole support if you really do want to fry and grill. In fact, teamed up with a tripod or camp crane, the backpacker with a trivet in their rucksack can cook almost anything over a fire.

**Advantages:** Simple. Depending on materials, can carry fairly heavy pots. Easy to use. Can often be created from materials found on site, and therefore suitable for the backpacker.

**Disadvantages:** Can only hold a single pot or pan easily. Only really suitable for boiling and general heating.

The cantilever or camp crane.

The horizontal pole system.

## Horizontal pole

This simple and elegant hanging system has the advantage of being able to carry more than one pot, although you obviously need to ensure the various elements are strong enough. One drawback, and a potential problem not often acknowledged in construction descriptions, is the difficulty that can be experienced in setting up the two ever so important Y-shaped uprights. If the traditional shape shown in most guidebooks is employed, the supports are frequently all but impossible to drive into the ground without damage. Burial of the bottom end is therefore required to ensure they remain stable and upright, and this is often a lot easier said than done. The key to easy horizontal pole setups is to choose the right shaped pieces of wood for these two supports.

As it's the perfect place to start, let's imagine we are in a hazel coppice. Rather than choosing the usual Y-shaped pole, depicted in so many drawings and photographs, search instead for a pole where a stout side-shoot has developed, leaving the main pole to continue upwards without any deviation. Once trimmed to shape, with a point at the base, these can be driven into the ground as easily as any standard stake.

If built properly, the horizontal pole makes a very versatile system, with few other pole-constructed supports able to carry more than one pot with such ease. Just ensure that the horizontal pole is high enough to avoid unwanted combustion. As with other systems, I prefer to use wire or chains and hooks to hold the cooking vessel in place, not least because they can be altered so easily to adjust pot height. If you don't have the required metal hanging bits and pieces, some form of wooden hooks can be rustled easily enough using local materials. I'll take a look at these after considering the single-pole crane, where they can be equally useful.

One key advantage, like the fire irons, is that heat in a pot can be reduced while cooking, simply by sliding it to one side.

**Advantages:** Simple. Robust. Suited to the backpacker as materials are often available in the wild. Can carry more than one pot. Easy to adjust cooking heat.

*Disadvantages:* Can be a little tricky to set up reliably if the right pair of uprights can't be found.

**Single pole crane**

I must admit I'm only including this system rather reluctantly. Despite its apparent simplicity, this is a pot support arrangement that needs to be constructed very carefully if failure isn't to be your camping companion. Then again, with only one pole needed, it is a very useful method for the backpacker, or anyone else wishing to travel light for that matter.

The emphasis when using a single pole crane, and not much of a surprise I suspect, is to ensure stability at the fixed end. Some people just use two stones, one to hold the bottom end, the other as a fulcrum. I suspect logs are often better, usually being less slippery, especially if a slot is cut in the fulcrum to avoid unwanted sideways movement. Ideally, the base is buried, ensuring it cannot move. The fulcrum stone or log should then be chosen with care to ensure it has a deep saddle or V, once again to hold the pole steady. It should go without saying that this fulcrum needs to sit in place securely too. You could use a short Y-shaped pole as a fulcrum of course, but then, I suppose, the arrangement wouldn't technically be a single pole crane anymore.

A notch cut in the top end of the stave will help keep the pot in place. You could of course hang your pot using a light hook and chain, as you would for some of the systems mentioned already. Alternatively, a beak-nosed wooden hanger can be used successfully, and more on that soon.

If the pot proves to be a little too heavy for the pole, a short stave, pointed at one end, with a natural Y shape at the other can be pushed or knocked into the ground to support the far end.

*Advantages:* Simple. Materials can usually be found on site, and therefore useful for the backpacker.

*Disadvantages:* Can be very unstable if not constructed with care.

The single pole crane, resting on a sturdy stone (with a good notch).

A short Y-shaped pole to add a little support.

How To Cook Using a Wood Fire

*The beak-nosed hanger in use, on the medium setting.*

## A beak-nosed hanger

While I find it easy and convenient to carry a length of galvanised wire from which to hang my pot, or a light chain and a couple of wire hooks, there may come a time when you just can't put a hand on a convenient piece when needed. Alternatively, and quite reasonably, you may feel that you'd prefer to stick to natural materials, found at each campsite, or wish to cut every gram or ounce from your loaded pack weight. This is where some form of wooden pot hanger comes to the fore.

These can also be very useful when hanging a pot at the end of a single pole crane, when you normally have no real control over its height, and therefore the heat. A wooden hanger works well with cantilever system too. In both cases though, care obviously needs to be taken to ensure they are fixed securely in place. The version I constructed should sort any stability problems out, and is often known as a beak-nosed hanger. The reason for the name should become clear.

To make one of these useful bits of kit, you'll need no more than a good sharp knife and a coppice or hedgerow. The ideal starting point is a hazel rod, about thumb thick, or a little thicker, that has split to grow a side shoot. Cut this away just below the divide. Now cut the thinner side shoot down to about thumb length. The main shoot can be cut to about as long as your arm. It should be obvious where the pot handle will sit.

The next bit is a little trickier, but shouldn't prove too difficult to master. The aim is to produce three or four notches along the longer length. Cut at points about an outstretched hand's breadth apart; these can be used to hang the hook at different heights over your fire.

To produce each notch, it is often easiest to start by cutting a cross at the desired point. Crucially, you need to make sure these are on the same side of the long stem as the side shoot. With the beaks cut here, any hanging arrangement will be much more stable than a setup that places them on the opposite side.

Cutting away wood on the hook side of the cross, a little beak can be produced. If this is undercut, as shown in the accompanying photo, it will stay in place much better. The photo also shows how the end of the single pole can be trimmed to produce a slight raised lip, increasing security further. The same system can be utilised with the camp crane. In either case, to adjust the heat in your pot, simply select a different beak.

This type of hanger can also be used with a horizontal pole, where a little trough, cut on the upper side of the supporting rod, will accommodate the beak safely. Alternatively, you could use a short section of wire as shown in the photo of the tripod/wooden hanger photo, simply hooked over the horizontal pole.

Left: cut a cross at the desired point.

Right: your beak should end up looking something like this.

Left: the hanger in place on the end of a single pole.

Right: the beak sat in a cut trough on a horizontal pole.

How To Cook Using a Wood Fire

The stick, in use.

## The stick

A simple stick can be surprisingly useful, and is the ideal system for the backpacking campfire cook looking for the lightest option. To picture the stick in use, I need only mention that old campfire cliché, the toasted marshmallow. For those not particularly taken by these gooey and very sweet balls, something rather more sustaining, such as humble toast, more ambitious bread, a fish, or in fact just about anything you can spear securely, can be cooked successfully at a sharpened end. One very distinct advantage of this hand-held system is that heat and resultant cooking rates can be adjusted simply and almost instantly. The trick is to keep any one side of your offering from lingering too close or for too long.

As with the single pole crane, a Y-shaped support can be pushed into the ground on the far side of the fire, easing whatever burden may be experienced.

Should the stick prove too tiresome to hold, or you could just do with your hands free, it can be stuck in the ground. In most instances the stick will be set at an angle to hold the offering to be cooked out over the fire, but it can also be set vertically to one side.

Positioned carefully, and with a watchful eye kept on developments, a surprising variety of foods can be cooked successfully like this, even whole salmon fillets or thin cuts, almost sheets, of meat. In these cases though, a slight elaboration, achieved by simply splitting the stick and clamping the fishy or meaty slice between the two halves, will probably make the whole attempt even more successful. You could even add thin horizontal stick struts to help hold things in place, but this is straying quite a way from the humble stick starting point.

*Advantages:* As simple as it could be. Materials can usually be found on site, and therefore ideal for the weight-conscious backpacker.

*Disadvantages:* Rather limited use (unless elaborated upon that is).

## Green log supports

Partly because it means cutting green wood, I tend to see this method of pot support as something of a backup system, used where materials for other techniques are simply not available. The other reason I relegate it to a reserve or emergency role, and have left its inclusion till this late in the list, is that I've never been much impressed by the results. On the other hand, all that's required are a pair of logs, about two to 60–90cm (2–3 feet) long, and about 15cm (6 inches) wide. These can then be placed parallel with each other, one to either side of the fire, the pots rested between them, much as you would with fire irons. If you can find them, two lengths of waterlogged dead stuff will do perfectly well too.

The advantage with this system is that nothing need be carried from site to site when travelling. The disadvantages, as I see it, other than the potential need to cut living wood, is that it can be hard to get at your fire, trapped as it is between the two flanking logs. This makes it tricky to add fuel and otherwise tend to your heat source. The two logs also cut down the opportunity for air to reach your fire, unless you prop the ends. Finally, because of the gap needed to provide room for a workable fire, and the curve of the logs, it is usually only possible to prop large-based vessels such as frying pans and large saucepans. Kettles, unless particularly big, will simply fall between the breach.

*Advantages:* Simple. Robust. Can carry heavy pots. Can support more than one vessel. Can often be created from materials found on site, and therefore suitable for the backpacker.

*Disadvantages:* Usually requires the cutting of green wood. Can only hold pans with a wide base. Hard to maintain and fuel the fire (which often doesn't burn too well due to restricted airflow).

A pair of green logs, used to support a large kettle. These are willow, so will hold out for quite a while.

How To Cook Using a Wood Fire

# Cooking

With the problem of how to support your pot over the fire solved, I hope, it's now a matter of how to produce a meal in them. It must be pretty obvious by now that Susannah and I have a preference for cooking over fire irons, so I'll start a discussion from this position. Many of the following comments will be just as relevant to cooking while employing other supports systems, but I'll try to ensure that any differences are made clear.

## Cooking over fire irons

Before your pot arrives, check that the irons are level, and about 5cm (2 inches) or so, maybe a little more, above the embers. At this height the bottom of the pan sits close enough to be heated easily, while still leaving room between the hot coals and the underside of the fire irons to add additional slim or thin-cut fuel.

The ember bed never needs to be much broader than the base of your cooking vessel.

One mistake that's often made, and not just when cooking with fire irons, is allowing a cooking fire to grow too big. If you think about it, the aim of the whole cooking process is to heat a pot or pan, so the bed of embers never needs to be more than a touch broader than the base of your cooking vessel. Any wider, and you not only waste fuel, but you end up cooking yourself too. As few pots have a bottom with a diameter more than 20–25cm (8–10 inches) that should be the limit of your fire's width.

It should extend a little along the line of the fire irons though – resulting in a sort of 'embery' lozenge about 30cm (12 inches) to 45cm (18 inches) in length. This not only means that you can add a second pan if needed, but this long bed also ensures that all-important control of the heat.

With a single pan or pot, one end of the elongated ember bed can be allowed to die back a bit (by stoking less frequently), while the other end is kept lively by stoking more often. The pan can then be slid to the lively end when more heat is needed, or to the quieter end to slow things down. It really is that simple. If things at the cooler end are still too warm, simply do as you would at home, and lift the pan away from the heat completely. Now, if one person concentrates on fire management, maintaining those embers, the other can just cook.

For quick frying and to bring water to the boil rapidly, just add more fuel and keep a lively flame going. You'll soon find you can heat things much faster like this than you ever could over any gas fire.

A slight cautionary note here. Don't get too carried away with that fuel. Add too much, especially if it arrives in large chunks, and you may well swamp things. You'll soon gain a feel for this, but a fire needs air and room for the flames to move as much as fuel, so a balance needs to be maintained to keep those hot coals going. If you do over-stoke a little, either lift some of the unlit fuel away, or just wait a while. Unless you've really smothered those embers, or the fire is still very young, everything will eventually wriggle back to life again.

*An elongated ember bed allows control over heat.*

How To Cook Using a Wood Fire

The other thing to consider, and it might seem slightly counterintuitive, is that small thin stuff, if stoked frequently, will produce much more heat than larger pieces of wood, at least in the short term. In fact, one way to slow things down for a while can be to add one or two heftier logs. Until they've caught fire themselves, they are really only barriers between pot and ember after all.

You'll also find that some fuel just burns better than others. With experience you may well know this before adding a twig from a particular tree to the fire, but surprises happen. In the end, experimentation on the day will soon tell you which wood is going to flare up and burn the moment it touches those embers, and which is going to sit there sullenly for the next five minutes before starting to burn. Each will have its use.

**Under a tripod, crane or pole**

Many of the comments made already about fire management and control under fire irons are just as valid if your pot is hung over it from a tripod, crane or horizontal pole. The fire only ever needs to be a little larger than the vessel itself, with perhaps an elongated shape developed to provide a hotter and cooler end. When using the crane or horizontal pole, the pot can be slid over or away from the heat as needed. Alternatively the height can be adjusted. Remember that even with a tripod, assuming it's not too hefty, the whole thing can be shifted carefully to one side to take a pot away from the heat.

One particular caution applies to the camp crane, and that concerns the structural integrity of the setup when the pot is lifted off its hook or chain. Much of the rigidity of the system relies on the weight provided by the pot at the end of the arm, quite simply forcing the hooked ends of the two outriggers tight against the upright support. Once that weight is removed, and the all-important friction reduced, there is a danger the whole thing will collapse. It doesn't always happen, but the possibility is worth bearing in mind.

## Grilling

Grilling over a wood fire is simplicity itself, and this is where the old wire oven shelf comes into its own. These can be propped on a few stones, but they're much more efficient if dropped onto those fire irons. You might push them apart a little first to provide a more stable base.

The most important thing for effective and controlled grilling is that good deep bed of embers. Only in very rare cases, and I'm thinking here of grilling perch for example (see chapter: What to Cook), will flame be a good idea. In brief, flames burn bare food, while embers cook it.

As for temperature control, the principle is just the same as described before. Assuming your ember bed is good and mature, it should be easy to ensure that one end is hotter than the other. To control the rate of your grilling, just move the food about.

Should everything die down to the point where the embers are not really doing the job anymore, just shuffle your food to one side, stoke over the embers at the other end, and wait until the resultant new outbreak of flame has burnt down again. This will now be your new hot end.

# Reflector oven

The proof, as they say, quite literally for a change, is in the pudding... and the puddings from a good reflector oven come out pretty darn well. As do baked mushrooms, loaves of bread, roasted potatoes, sausages or roasted vegetables. We've cooked dozens of different dishes, ranging from hot sticky cakes to roast beetroot and baked fish. It's all pretty simple, especially on the oven side of the equation. With heat arriving from all angles any tray or pan need only be turned occasionally to provide some impressively even results.

Using an old wire oven shelf to grill, in this case propped over fire irons. Note that the fire has been raised off the underlying damp ground using stone slabs.

Using our Svante Fredén reflector oven in an appropriate setting.

You can see the all important angled sides reflecting the heat on this purpose built Svante Fredén oven.

The fire doesn't need to be big; it just needs a few flames. This fire is divided to boil water while baking. Note the fire bowl in the background.

To obtain the best outcomes when in use, the oven needs to be pretty much on the same level as the fire, close, but not so near that the base becomes overlain with embers (when I understand there's a chance it can deform or even melt when trying to obtain high temperatures).

To my eye, this really shouldn't happen. From our experience, the fire doesn't need to be either large or unwieldy to produce some perfectly usable cooking temperatures in the oven, and quickly too. Even with a fire not much bigger than a dinner plate, and not lit for more than ten minutes or so, we've had cooking oil bubbling merrily around potatoes almost as soon as the roasting dish was placed on its wire seat.

Unlike traditional wood-fire cooking, when best results are obtained after developing a good deep bed of glowing embers, the heat captured by the reflector oven is from the flames. Using good dry twigs and thinly spit logs, those flames can be at work immediately. If less heat is needed, you slow the rate of stoke. When more is required, you simply feed them into the burning pile a little quicker.

While it is undoubtedly easier to cook using a fire to heat the oven on its own, we've frequently managed to combine reflector oven management with a pot or grill shelf propped on our fire irons. It isn't particularly tricky to manipulate a fire to display a duel personality; an ember rich patch lying under the pot, pan or grilling area, while a patch of flame dances merrily off to the side facing the open oven. Cod and roast potatoes, cooked at the same time on the northern Norwegian coast, stands out as a particularly enjoyable meal from a dual use campfire.

One small matter to consider; make sure the inside of your oven is kept clean. Sitting close to the fire, with smoke often swirling inside, the reflective inner surfaces can slowly become quite sooty, significantly reducing the efficiency of the oven. Gentle cleaning, that avoids scratching the fairly soft aluminium sides, will make a pretty dramatic difference to cooking times. I haven't yet gone as far as polishing the inside of my oven, but suspect a bit of a shine would make quite a difference too.

# Dutch ovens

These admittedly rather heavy items of kit offer the distinct benefit of versatility. Used as a large saucepan, you can simmer and boil as usual, but food can also be placed inside that solid cast iron lump to roast and bake.

When cooking casseroles or stews, the Dutch oven is really no different to any pan. Just hang or prop it (using a sturdy support system) over your fire. A major difference is that you can sit your oven straight onto the embers if you wish. Most pots or pans don't care too much for this, but a Dutch oven will be fine – usually. I would advise though, if the weather is particularly chilly, not to swing your oven off the cold ground, and certainly not off the snow, and straight onto a hot fire. The cast iron just might not be able to take that rapid and extreme change in temperature.

The main departure from normal pot use is that you can bury your Dutch oven in the embers of your fire, even heaping them over the lid. The better Dutch ovens have a high lip around the edge of the lid just to hold these embers in place. With the heat from these burning coals coming at the food inside from all angles, a very even cooking environment can be produced, perfect for roasting and baking. However, the whole process does need a little thought and care.

I began this chapter by stressing the importance of temperature control in wood-fired cooking, and this is just as important here, only a little trickier to judge. With the food sealed within your oven, it isn't immediately visible. As a result the most common problem experienced by people experimenting with Dutch oven cooking is burning the contents. The key to avoiding this is to always err on the side of having everything a little too cool than a little too hot. After all, there's almost always a fairly simple response to an undercooked dish, but rarely anything that can be done with burnt food other than cutting away the most charred and inedible bits.

Setting out to roast or bake results in the only occasion when I'll build a fairly big fire, dropping some pretty hefty logs, maybe three to 8–10cm (4 inches) wide, onto the fire. I'll then let these burn through almost completely to produce a good

*You can hang or prop a Dutch oven (using a sturdy support system) over your fire.*

Look closely, and you can see a pair of six-inch nails, used to lift the loaf tin off the base of the oven.

deep bed of glowing ember lumps. Softwoods such as pine or spruce tend to burn through too quickly, and the best embers will definitely develop with a hardwood fuel. While all this is happening, I also place the oven on the fire for a short while, just to warm it all through. Try not to leave it there too long though, as it can be very easy to carbonise any natural protective coating that has developed over the inner surface through use.

Once the flames have all died down, and the embers are just sitting there, glowing a little more brightly every time a breeze wafts through, I use a stick to clear a space at the centre of this bed, leaving only a thin layer of crushed embers over an area a few inches wider than the base of the pot. This is where you'll sit your oven.

It's still very hard to judge the temperature, but if I can hold an open palm about 20cm (8 inches) above this area for three seconds or more, it's probably not too hot. It should go almost without saying that this test has to be approached with care.

When baking, it's perfectly possible to place your cake or loaf directly on the base of the oven, but I prefer to use some form of tin or other container that will help keep the food from touching the hot inside edges. If you take care not to leave too deep a bed of embers beneath your oven, the base rarely grows hot enough to burn food easily, often cooking the base of a pie or loaf perfectly, for example. One trick to avoid this possibility, until you have a good feel for the whole process, is to place your baking tin on something to raise it up a little. I carry a pair of six-inch nails, but you could use anything that will take the heat and not taint the food.

Many people also grow a little too enthusiastic about the number of embers placed on the lid, with inevitable results. Again, any advice about the right amount is hard to quantify, but keep in mind that it will always be better to have too few lumps of glowing charcoal up top than too many.

When cooking with embers on the lid, the heat produced within the pot can be slightly uneven. To counteract this, you can either move the embers about a little, or more easily, just rotate the lid a little every few minutes. Many people carry some sort of stout bent wire hook to lift the lid. As I usually have a pair of pliers in my camping make and mend bag, I tend to use these. They do provide a good solid hold, but it is best to wear a pair of gloves, as your hand does end up pretty close to the heat. Turning the whole oven on its ember bed, using the main wire handle, will also help in heating the interior of the oven evenly.

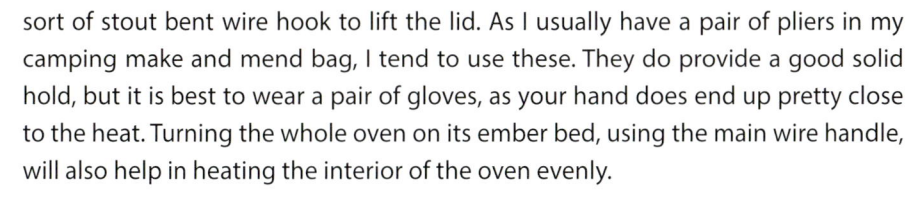

Left: using a pair of pliers, and a leather glove, to rotate the lid on a Dutch oven.

Right: the lid of a Dutch oven, covered in gently glowing embers.

## Muurikka and fire bowls

As they share many features, we can take a look at cooking with Muurikka and fire bowls together.

In many ways the fire bowl, or a large Muurikka used as a fire bowl, is really no different from a cooking fire in a shallow scoop on a beach or in the woods. Once lit, and then allowed to mature, you can use them to cook in just the same way, supporting your pots and pans over the top with fire irons, a tripod, camp crane,

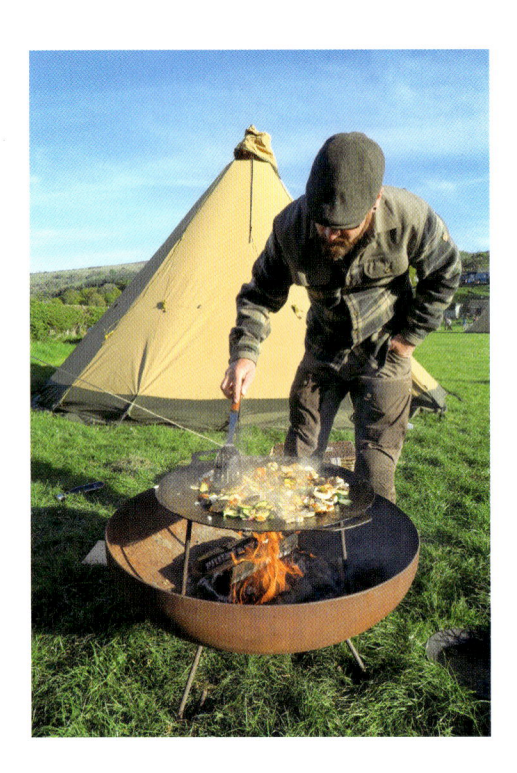

A Muurikka in use over a large fire bowl.

or whatever other method you choose. A Dutch oven will sit inside perfectly happily, or can be suspended overhead by something robust. Perhaps only the reflector oven would present a few challenges, but even these could almost certainly be overcome with a little ingenuity.

Of course the Muurikka (or griddle pan) can also be used directly over the fire as a cooking vessel in its own right. And a fine one it is too, allowing frying, dry-roasting, simmering and boiling within its shallow open bowl. Through basic manipulation of the underlying fire, warmer and cooler spots can be created within the bowl, or the fire can simply be kept small, which is my preference, when a cooler periphery surrounds a hot centre. Not only can this edge be perfect when high cooking temperatures would spoil food, but is perfect for keeping cooked food warm until everything is ready to serve. For all these reasons, one of the larger Muurikkas is often worth the extra weight and resultant difficulty in transport.

What's more, the Muurikka you're cooking in can be propped for use in either a fire bowl, or just another Muurikka, usually a larger one. In Finland, where campfires often need to be kept off the ground, this double-Muurikka system is very popular, with many Finns able to conjure up some wonderfully varied dishes using this simple system.

## After the meal

### Washing up

If there is any food left on plates or in bowls, and this is almost unknown in the Gent camp, the remains can usually be burnt on the fire. Before we set forth to clean them further, we usually use paper kitchen roll, or leaves, to wipe away just about anything left, with the dirty results going on the fire too. All this means that when it comes to actually washing things, little soap or water is needed.

Some form of detergent is usually required though, and we use biodegradable versions in as small amounts as possible. Water might be collected from a stream, lake or the sea, but any dirty or soapy results are discarded at a reasonable distance to reduce the chance of contamination. Only when the plates, bowls or pans are clean, might they be rinsed off.

If you run out of soap, or are really keen to keep pack weights down, a little of the grey fluffy wood ash, mixed with water, makes a powerful detergent. Be very careful though, the resultant mush is also extremely alkaline, and could cause serious damage to your skin if left in contact for long. Above all, do everything you can to keep it away from your eyes.

Cleaning the soot off a pan with wet sand.

## Cleaning your pots and pans

Cleaning pots and pans is no different to sprucing up the plates, mugs and bowls, just a dirtier job that usually takes quite a bit longer. Once again, but with all the warnings just given, if your cooking vessels are really greasy, or coated with baked-on food, that wet wood ash will usually shift it, although you might need to leave it sitting there for a little while to do its magic.

One trick we have developed, or rather Susannah has developed, deals with the baked-on fire residue on the outside of pans. Now I have to admit, that left to my own devices, I'd probably leave it there, but this sooty black and slightly greasy layer does tend to migrate. What were once pristine trousers or sleeping bags can soon look pretty grubby after only fleeting contact with a well-used pan.

Using just the water and sand often found somewhere along a beach, lake edge or river bank, Susannah sits and rocks the pot exterior back and forth in this abrasive mix. Ideally this is done right at the water's edge, where the effect is most apparent. No detergent is used, so nothing other than carbon should be entering the water, and in these amounts we believe that no harm is done. We certainly have some very clean pots and pans, and we've even been accused of using only brand new kit before now. One observer, seeing our sparkly stainless MSR pot collection, and looking really quite pleased with his exposé, suggested that we obviously didn't cook over a fire as often as we claimed.

How To Cook Using a Wood Fire   125

Many a fine camp meal starts by frying onions.

126   What Food To Take, and How To Take It

# What Food To Take, and How To Take It

Once all the kit is in place, and the cooking gear is sorted out for the journey, you need to consider what food you are going to take. In many ways this should be a pretty easy decision, without need of assistance. Much of it will be down to personal preference after all. However, some raw materials are better suited for transportation and camp cooking than others, particularly with the intention to cook over a wood fire, so this chapter considers the ingredients we've found best suited to a sortie into the wild.

There is more to all this than just those raw materials of course, so along the way, the best methods to pack different sorts of food will also be discussed. In the next chapter, I'll offer some recipes that have been devised over time to best match this rewarding culinary method.

## Ingredients

Following a fair bit of experience, I'd hope the following suggestions are pretty sound, but if you fancy taking something else, and it fits in and won't overload whatever transport system you have in place, please don't be put off adding them to your list. All this camping and cooking stuff should be about personal fulfilment after all, rich with experimentation.

So what do we take?

*The start to some sort of interesting meal, with olive oil stored in a lightweight plastic bottle.*

*Our favourite way to take cooking oil into the wild.*

## Oils and fats

Both Susannah and I really like olive oil, so we carry it with us on our canoe camping trips, usually decanted into a small plastic bottle. Whatever vegetable oil you prefer can be taken in the same way, either carried in the original container, or in something smaller and lighter. Oil is pretty heavy stuff though, so try not to fall for the temptation of carrying too much – unless you have the supporting system to carry it all happily of course.

We also take butter, with the knowledge that the more salt it contains, the longer it will stay fresh, even if it might not be quite so good for cooking.

One disadvantage of olive oil, or any vegetable oil for that matter, lies in its tasty liquid state. Great in the bottle, not so wonderful each year or so when it manages to escape. There is an alternative though, and a while back we discovered coconut oil, and while this too can be fluid, this state tends to be less likely in the cooler conditions we often experience in north-west Europe. While the jar might be heavy, and no good for the backpacker, we do find the contents useful.

And so to Susannah's favourite camping oil, which forms part of a pack of Tropical Sun Premium Creamed Coconut. This remarkably useful stuff comes in tough meal-sized plastic bags that contain both coconut milk and oil in a solid 200g (7oz) block, the pale beige coloured creamed coconut filling about two thirds, the remaining section packed with opaque oil. Not only are these small packages a great way to carry coconut oil, but they can also assist admirably in the cooking of both curries and puddings.

For the backpacker looking for a little variety in their cooking methods, hoping perhaps to add a little frying to the repertoire, these little plastic wrapped blocks would be well worth the slight additional weight. No bottle or heavy carton is involved, and that cardboard outer box can always be dumped straight away to lose a few extra grammes. You also have creamed coconut to enliven a meal too.

### Flour, rice, pasta, lentils, and oats

Each of these staples, including quinoa, have their place in our provisions, and each are pretty bulky. They also need to be kept dry and free from rodent attack.

Unopened plastic bags of pasta, lentils and rice are usually fine, but once dipped into, each will be stored either in a dry bag or in one of our many clip-lock plastic boxes. In fact, because of the fairly disastrous results from getting it even a little damp, the flour goes into one of these protective systems even before it's opened.

When it comes to oats, I can't really imagine a camping trip where, packed away somewhere safe and dry, they didn't form part of our vital victual stores. Apart from tasting great, in our view anyway, the slow energy release characteristics of oats are perfectly in tune with the demands of a full day on the move.

### Beans

While we might carry a tin or two of cooked beans for those dark evenings when we just want to eat quickly, transported in this way this versatile foodstuff is overly heavy. Another consideration is that after the contents have been wolfed down, we'll also be left with that bulky empty can.

For these reasons, we usually carry our beans uncooked and dry. Where time and foresight allows, these will be soaked for 6 to 12 hours, and then boiled for a while. We've paddled quite some distances before now with a clip locked plastic box filled with water, rehydrating haricot, cannellini or black beans.

### Vegetables

We admit it, we carry an awful lot of vegetables with us, and are frequently thankful for the impressive haulage capacities of our canoe. In the end, the pattern of consumption is pretty standard, with those vegetables possessing a short shelf life,

Rice and bread flour, stored safely.

Beans soaking during a journey.

What Food To Take, and How To Take It

such as mushrooms and spinach, eaten soon after setting out, while the hardy stuff like the potatoes and leeks hang about to form the foundations for meals well into the latter stages of the trip.

I guess if there was one vegetable we really would be unhappy to set forth without, it would be the onion. We select only the firmest and brightest for the journey. Because we rarely seem to eat a meal without it, and because they are good travellers, bulbs of garlic are usually found a place too. Fresh ginger is unlikely to be left behind either.

Part of a vegetable haul.

### Fruit

This section could be transposed almost directly from the vegetable paragraph above, with the soft stuff, if we are lucky enough to find it, consumed first (and I can't hep thinking here of Spanish peaches and apricots), and the apples, for example, left till last.

### Fish

After thinking about it for a while, I can't ever recall having set out to camp while carrying fish, at least not fresh fish. With its very short shelf life, and well-recorded hygiene risks if allowed to sit around somewhere warm for too long, fish doesn't make the ideal camp store filler. We do eat quite a bit though (as you will probably deduce from the recipes in the next chapter).

Where it's allowed, we catch our own fish; where not, we go without. Apart from tinned tuna that is.

### Meat

We don't often take meat with us either, at least not as a raw commodity. Partly this is due to the fact that we don't find we miss it much out there, but also because, like fish, the risks of food poisoning from unrefrigerated meat are much higher than with vegetables or rice.

Where it's allowed, we catch our own.

130   What Food To Take, and How To Take It

En route, and where possible, we have been known to pull ashore to buy provisions, especially if something intriguing such as reindeer mince is for sale, but this is rare. It's a long time since I last snared a rabbit, although this option to provide fresh meat might appeal to some. Snares are very light to carry after all, and pretty effective if you know how and where to set them (oh, and where it's legal in the places you camp). Some canoe campers, where it's allowed, will even carry a shotgun to add the occasional duck or grouse to the repertoire.

What we will often carry is cured sausage such as Spanish chorizo. This has a good shelf life, plenty of nutrition for its relatively small size, and can add a surprising amount of flavour for its pack weight. French saucisson is also a fairly frequent camping companion, with smoked bacon carried at times due to its good lasting powers and flavour.

For the omnivorous backpacker, one of the best additions to any food collection must be that chorizo, or is that just my prejudices being revealed. Whatever, I'd still argue that those curled collections of compact flavour and sustenance are well worth the additional weight; and if they ever prove to be too bulky or heavy, you can always eat some.

A chorizo, or most of one.

## Eggs

People often avoid taking eggs on camping trips, fearing what they believe will be the inevitable breakages. It's not a problem we encounter often. Kept in their half-dozen sized cardboard boxes, and stored somewhere solid and unlikely to be sat upon, they're usually fine.

Even un-chilled eggs can last pretty well too, so long as they're fresh when bought that is. If you do expect to be out in the wild for long, and would like to have eggs on hand for a while, then the old trick of rolling each egg in melted butter to seal the shells, can help to keep bacteria out, and prolong their life considerably.

Kept in their half-dozen sized cardboard box.

It's also worth knowing that you only have to place your egg in a bowl or jug of water to check its freshness. A good egg will sit resolutely at the bottom of the container.

What Food To Take, and How To Take It

If it lifts at one end, but keeps the other on the base, it's on the turn, but probably ok. Only if your egg floats do you know the little stink bomb is well worth avoiding.

Of course, eggs do weigh a fair bit, and take up a lot of room. For the backpacker, the only real alternative, other than the odd original wrapped carefully and slipped in somewhere safe, is to use dried egg powder. When travelling under leg power alone, we just go without.

## Bread

All sorts of bread have been hauled by us out into the wild over the years; pain de campagne in the Pyrenees, rye bread in Slovenia, even some very odd liquorice-flavoured stuff from a well-provisioned store in northern Sweden, the name of the town dusted in flour on top (Susannah liked it).

Off course, most 'carried in' loaves need to be eaten fairly soon. We cook some of our own to maintain a fresh supply, but have found that in Scandinavia (and no doubt elsewhere too), it is very easy to buy either the traditional Swedish flat crispread, or stout paper bags of small dried loaves, already cut in half and ready for a topping. These last for ages unopened, and tend to be eaten well before softening once the seal is broken. These little loaves are also great for producing breadcrumbs when needed.

## Spices

All manner of powders, seeds and odd bits of bark are stored in little watertight plastic pots when we travel. When vehicle supported, and that includes the canoe, these will always include salt and black pepper (often each in their own grinder), and usually ground turmeric, cayenne and/or chilli flakes, paprika, ground cumin and ground coriander. Solid versions of cumin, coriander, which we'll grind lightly in camp, are not at all rare, and our whole spice collection will often include cinnamon, cloves and cardamom.

Whether you consider them vegetables or spices, we also carry fairly hefty supplies of garlic and ginger too.

*Liquorice-flavoured bread, hauled into the wild.*

*A mobile spice collection, the pepper in a plastic bottle with built-in grinder lid (admittedly it could be smaller).*

132  What Food To Take, and How To Take It

## Stock

Camping life must have been made so much easier when some creative soul invented the stock cube. We never set out into the wild without them, or at least something very similar, as a few years ago we discovered those little individual sealed pots of jellied stock. These are so easy to use, and often taste rather better than the traditional cube. I suspect most of ours are chicken or vegetable, but I see they now come in surprising variety. A few are even spiced, so I guess that could simplify stores for some.

*Sealed pots of jellied stock.*

## Nuts and seeds

Light, tasty and easy to store, we often carry walnuts and cashews. Depending on what we might cook, other nuts may come along for the journey too.

Although they're not really nuts, both desiccated and flaked coconut make useful and delicious additions to a number of meals, and weigh next to nothing. The coconut flakes make an appearance in one of the recipes described later, along with pumpkin seeds, which also often find a corner in our wannigan.

Last but not least, and possibly the most expensive item to accompany us regularly into the wild – pine nuts.

## Jars and bottles

Along with the carefully packaged, dry bagged and boxed raw ingredients, we do take a few processed things into the wild. We often use that canoe after all, and the small collection of resultant bottles and jars are usually pretty easy to carry, until that unexpected quarter mile portage (carry) around a surprisingly wild section of river! Some of the contained liquids and pastes really do make quite a difference.

I suppose one of the key things I'm saying here, is that if you really enjoy versatility and experimentation in your camp cooking, and if you have the ability to take it

A collection of jars, bottles and cans, found in our wannigan.

Collecting lingonberries in northern Sweden.

easily and without compromising fun or safety, then take what you like. A large 4x4, truck or even canoe can carry a surprising amount, stashed away carefully.

Depending on your camping meal preferences, and possible views about simplicity, some of the foods carried in like this may be met with nods of approval, others by complete bafflement. But that's the joy of all this, you can take what you want. In addition to the ingredients listed above, we will often carry vinegar, usually cider vinegar, and tamari, a variety of soy sauce. As they appear in many dishes we produce, we also often carry a jar of tahini and some Thai curry paste. The curry paste can often be bought in plastic sachets, although these can be difficult to seal safely, once opened (and the contents of a whole sachet, used in one go, can be scary... and yes, we've tried it). Sun-dried tomatoes can also be fun, and figure in one recipe in the next chapter.

**Found food**

Not only do Susannah and I enjoy setting out with a rod, or more often a handline, to catch fish, and relish the chance to harvest things like shellfish and seaweed from the rocks at low tide; we also enjoy foraging on land.

Probably our most frequent haul, seasons allowing, will be berries; wild blueberries, raspberries, strawberries and redcurrants, and the almost fabled Arctic cloudberry feature regularly in our meals. We also collect nuts, and pick quite a few plants, either to add flavour, such as wild fennel, or in the case of samphire, for example, as a main ingredient for a dish in itself.

We collect mushrooms too, but not that many, and it is here that I would like to raise a particular caution. There are dozens and dozens of different wild mushroom varieties out there, and we probably eat about six. I could probably choose about another dozen with almost complete confidence, but almost complete is just not nearly good enough. Many mushrooms will make you regret that meal for a few days. Some of course will kill you. And if that last sentence looks a bit brutal, it's meant to be. I've been poisoned by mushrooms, and these were served by people who claimed to know what they were doing. Thankfully, this resulted in no more than a particularly unpleasant night of vomiting and rather disagreeable hallucinations. So-called experts die every year.

Of course all this poison scare stuff is probably old news to you, and possibly rather a bore to read, but then I hope you'd agree that it would be utterly irresponsible of me not to mention it.

Wild food, found, collected and cooked yourself, can be a joy in so many ways, and we do offer a couple of recipes later that include them. However... if you have any doubts about your potential haul, whether it's a mushroom, a leaf or a berry, please leave it well alone.

To aid in identification in the following chapter, and help avoid perhaps costly mistakes, I've used what I believe to be the current Latin taxonomic names whenever wild foods are first mentioned.

A lovely cep, or Karl Johan, found in central Sweden.

Cloudberry picking in Finland.

What Food To Take, and How To Take It

Our wannigan.

# Storage

I've mentioned watertight plastic boxes and pots, and various bottles and bags already, and hopefully stressed their usefulness and versatility. Almost all of these fit neatly into our food box, or wannigan as it is often known in Canada, taken from one of the indigenous languages. This box is pretty big, but fits neatly amidships in our canoe, or in the back of the van, and carries most of the food we'll need for a camping trip.

There's no doubt that we often get a little carried away in the nearest store to our launch point, and anything that won't fit in is simply carried in additional plastic carrier bags. While these may seem environmentally unfriendly, the fact that they are subsequently employed to carry out all our rubbish should make up for it, we hope.

For backpacking trips, our food, however it might be wrapped individually, usually goes into a single lightweight dry bag, or rather two bags, one to carry each. These hold all your victuals in one place, and should keep any sensitive ingredients from getting damp (or falling prey to ants or other insects). Using a bag in a distinctive colour makes finding them easy when we're hungry, particularly as we like to pack other items such as food, cooking gear and first aid materials in individual bags as well. We tend to store a few snacks in the rucksack lid for quick and easy access.

Storing food in a dry bag would be a good option for the kayaker or cyclist too, although with slightly less concern about weight, a bag in a heavier fabric might be a good idea. Mind you, the colour-coding idea is almost certainly worth sticking with.

# How much food to take

Working out what food to take can be fun. Trying to decide how much to pack can be a little more nerve-wracking.

We find the best approach is to break everything down to the individual meal. So for example if you're setting out for four days, that's four breakfasts, four lunches and four dinners. Multiplying that by the number of campers, in our case usually two, and we know we need to cater, quite literally, for eight of each. It's then down to experience.

We tend to eat much the same thing for breakfast each day, usually some form of oat-based muesli. This bit is easy then, and a 1kg bag of oats will usually last us both a week. When backpacking, to keep weight down, and because it also simplifies things in camp, we will often prepare and pre-pack a breakfast each for each day, using small reusable plastic freezer bags for light storage. This might make quite a good move for the cyclist or kayaker.

It's then a case of thinking through each remaining meal, and ensuring that the required ingredients are packed away in the wannigan. This might seem rather time consuming, but it is far better than going hungry, and besides, it isn't as tricky or longwinded as it sounds.

The other trick is to always err on the overdoing it side of any doubt. It really is, after all, much better to return with enough for a couple more meals, than to go hungry. Of course if space or weight is at a premium, the balance will need to be more carefully judged.

You're also never going to regret throwing in a couple of 'emergency' bars of chocolate... just in case.

*Just some of the food we might take canoe camping, but how long will it last?*

*This collection of dehydrated meals might last a backpacker for days.*

What Food To Take, and How To Take It    137

Dehydrated vegetables, stored for use in a stew.

## Dehydrator

What seems like quite a long way back now, I mentioned our food dehydrator. Having just presented this discussion about careful selection, I will now seem to ignore all that by suggesting that with one of these impressive machines pressed into service before you set out, almost any food can be taken into the wild, by just about any traveller.

Sealed in an airtight plastic bag or box, it can then be pulled from your food box or rucksack, and rehydrated over a wood fire with the minimum of effort and time. Hearty stews can be followed by sweet fruity puddings, each packed with all the calories you are likely to have burnt off during the day.

For these reasons alone, just about the single best move a campfire cooking backpacker might make, would be to buy a dehydrator. An assortment of ultra-light and easy to store bags of dry food will be available at little cost and with relatively little effort, ensuring that even the most weight conscious pedestrian traveller, or any other form of traveller for that matter, will be able to take a range of good things into the wild to cook over a wood fire. This isn't cheating. This is just plain good sense. You will still be using a fire to bring that meal bag to life after all.

## Final thoughts

For many people, and for varying reasons, their time in the wild is not about the finer points of eating. While trying to get to the top of something high, or crossing something fast, and with the exception of calorie counts and energy release characteristics, the focus and goal for the trip will lie elsewhere. I have nothing against this. We've travelled the same way ourselves after all. But if your reason for wilderness living is to really experience the space your moving through, then there is no reason to have to accept a hurried meal. Cooking can be treated as one of the key events. Unless you are rushing around, and I might suggest rushing around a little too much, you really should have the time available to make the most of your time around the fire in the evening. These are the hours in which you can cook old favourites, and experiment with new dishes, unexpected 'found' ingredients, or new cooking techniques.

When camping, Susannah and I certainly see no reason why we shouldn't be able to cook properly. In fact, we don't see why we shouldn't eat just as well, sometimes even a little better, than we do at home. For us, camp cooking is about more than just getting by, simply making the best of what some may perceive as a somewhat tricky situation, with limitations imposed by the setting. Instead, we look forward to benefitting from what we consider to be the many advantages out there, in being rewarded by those circumstances because what's on offer when cooking over a wood fire in the wild is so good.

Besides, by slowing up enough to give all this a proper go, collecting tinder from one copse, fuel from another, perhaps gathering driftwood from along the high tide line of a beach, we have the chance to become truly immersed in the environment we're visiting. Because of the way we choose to cook we will be interacting with the trees that have lived at this spot after all, living here for tens, even hundreds of years. They will provide the heat. We will benefit, and then offer their nutrients back to the soil. By adding to a dish by a little foraging and gleaning, some of those nutrients will end up in you, the energy collected here from the sun and the local geology used by your body to continue your exploration. As well as being fun, satisfying and often deeply rewarding, cooking over a wood fire is the perfect way not only get to know where you have chosen to set up your temporary kitchen and home, but in a small way to become part of it, and it part of you.

A chance to become truly immersed in the environment.

Better than watching television.

140   What To Cook

# What To Cook

After all the discussion of wood types, fire lighting methods, responsible campfire management and food selection, here, at last, is the cooking bit, with our ideas for the meals you can bring to life over your flame and embers.

Of course just about anything you might choose to prepare at home can be cooked in camp. It's true that some dishes, the ones involving baking and roasting for example, might be a touch tricky, but even these can usually be accomplished over a fire with a little patience and ingenuity. A few of these more difficult culinary challenges, such as bread making, are tackled below. There seems little point however in producing a recipe section in a campfire cooking book that simply trots out a list of meals just because they are good to eat. Providing a recipe for say spaghetti Bolognese, before adding helpfully that you can cook it over a fire, is of little use to most aspiring camp cooks. Instead, in setting out the following recipes, I've made a conscious attempt to present dishes that are different, either because they are cooked over a wood fire or because they have been altered to suit this method.

I admit that some dishes do rather fall outside this bracket. So others have been chosen for their particular character. There is nothing fundamentally different for example about our pancake recipe from the one we would use at home. However this recipe, and a few others, are so well suited to the whole wood fire thing, and we cook this dish so often, that we felt they had to be included. Besides, our pancakes are so frequently cooked with the addition of blueberries or wild raspberries, fresh from the woods nearby, that perhaps it is reasonable to claim they are suitably campfire evolved anyway.

Filled to normal drinking levels, my plastic cup takes 300ml (half a pint).

Where the dish isn't in itself particular to wood-fired methods, it may be the ingredients that merit its inclusion. These should have proven themselves by being ideally suited to camping storage and transportation, as well as being well-matched for eventual cooking over burning wood, or simply available from the woods, beach or water nearby.

Alternatively, it may be the cooking methods themselves that have earned them a place, and at least two meals have been included because, despite being fairly complex in flavour and texture, they are produced easily in a single pan. A couple of meals are included on the grounds that they allow for a slightly more involved method to be explored more closely.

And yes, maybe one or two recipes have been included simply because we like them.

## Measurements

As it's extremely unlikely that anyone is going to lug a set of scales into the wild, it will be hard to find any weights given in the following recipes. Instead, amounts are listed in teaspoons, tablespoons, or mugs (as you are likely to be carrying them). When spoons are used to measure dry goods, these will be heaped unless stated otherwise.

For most recipes it is the ratio of ingredients in the mix that's more important than the individual amounts, so the size of the mug itself is not too important, but we would expect one to hold something between 280–340g (10–12oz).

A few liquid measurements are given, as it is possible for many to carry some form of measuring jug. Alternatively, it isn't hard to find out how much one of your mugs holds before you set out. Filled to normal drinking levels, mine takes 300ml (half a pint) for example.

Following these guidelines you are much more likely to find such scientifically specific guidance as a small lump, a dollop, a smear or a few drops. As campers, and therefore intelligent and adaptable folk, I have every confidence that this imprecision will be just fine.

What To Cook

# Recipes

The following recipes have been divided into four sections. In turn, these offer cooking suggestions for bread, little meals and side dishes (including a couple of snacks), big meals and finally puddings. In the big meal section the fish dishes, and there are quite a few, have been huddled together in a shoal.

On the whole, unless the amounts of the key ingredients are obviously flexible, each recipe will cater for two campers.

Happy cooking.

Dinner, cooked over wood collected from the beach.

What To Cook  143

This brown reflector oven loaf was baked on a Swedish island, close to the Arctic Circle.

## Bread

### *Reflector oven loaf*

Most campers have a particular meal or food type they miss while camping, one that is easy to prepare or store at home, but they feel just doesn't really fit in on the trail. For many, that's a good loaf of bread.

A Dutch oven can be pressed into use pretty successfully, and many a decent loaf has emerged from one over the years. As we are not able to see what's going on in there, temperature control can however be a little hit and miss at times. This is where a good reflector oven comes into its own. Everything happens right in front of you, and not only is this fun (who needs television?), it is also simplicity itself to adjust the heat experienced by that gently browning crust.

This basic loaf recipe has been designed specifically for the Svante Fredén oven – but only because the amounts have been adjusted to suit a tin size that fits best. In all other aspects, this is the loaf we'd bake at home. It would just be about two or three times the size cooked there.

Ingredients:
- 1½ mugs strong white bread flour or wholemeal bread flour
- Teaspoon dry yeast powder (we've found Allinson's works very well, and the little yeast balls come in a great little waterproof tin – which has many recycled uses amongst our camping kit once empty)
- Teaspoon salt
- About ½ to ⅔ mug water
- A few drops of vegetable oil, or a smear of butter

Kit:
- Svante Fredén reflector oven
- ½lb bread tin

**To cook:**

Warm the water in a kettle (if you are unable hold your fingers comfortably in the water, it's too hot). Add to the yeast, give it a good stir and then leave to sit for five minutes or so.

Add the salt to the flour.

Once the yeast is active (it will probably be frothing or bubbling slightly), give it another good stir then add this water/yeast mix to the flour and mix everything roughly with a spoon.

Tip it all out onto a plastic cutting board or clean plank and mix and knead by hand. This will take about five to ten minutes, folding the mix itself (no need for pressing in my book). The aim here is to add air, not to push it out. When the dough is smooth and springy, put it in a bowl and cover while it rises. Depending how warm it is, this will take from one to three hours or so.

Once the dough has at least doubled in size, smear some oil or butter thinly over the inside of your baking tin, and shake in a little flour to coat this layer. This should stop the loaf sticking in there. Then take your dough, squash it flat, fold it into a short sausage shape, and lay this along the bottom of the tin. Place this somewhere away from drafts to rise again. We often use our wannigan.

Once the dough has at least doubled again, place your reflector oven alongside a lit and mature fire. Keeping an eye on the dough to ensure it doesn't brown too quickly, stoke for a constant low to medium temperature, turning the tin once or twice until the dough has risen, and the top has gained a golden brown colour. This will take anywhere between half an hour to an hour.

Once cooked, knock out the loaf. A tap on the bottom will tell you if it's done (an uncooked loaf feels and sounds stodgy) then try to prop it up off the ground or cooking area, to let the air in and cool it. And there you are.

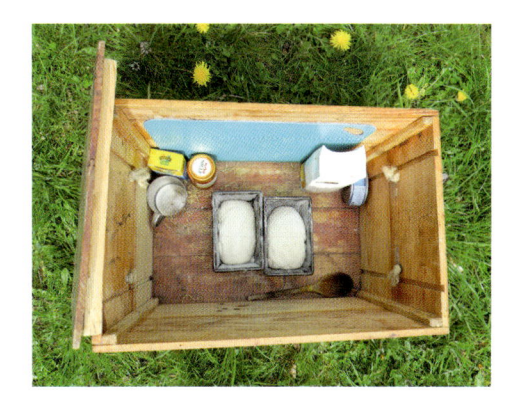

A couple of loaves, placed in our nearly emptied wannigan to rise for the second time.

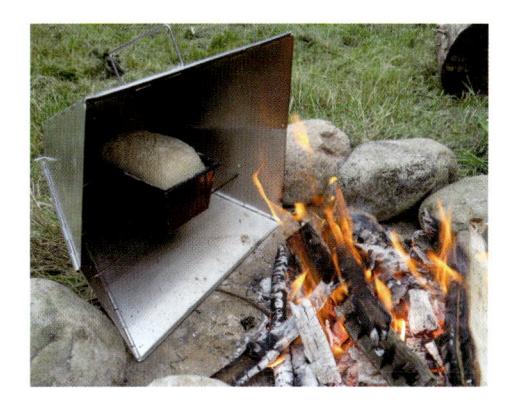

Just beginning to brown.

Bannock.

*Bannock*

As I admitted in my book *Canoe Camping*, you just can't write about camp cooking without addressing the risky matter of bannock. I say risky, because no matter what recipe I might choose to suggest, a whole swathe of experienced camp cooks, from Brisbane to Banff, are going to be absolutely adamant I have it all wrong. In fact, while writing *Canoe Camping* I almost chickened out. It really was only at the last minute (I think the publisher's comment went something along the lines of 'Go on, take it on the chin') that I provided the following simple version.

I suspect this is pretty close to the variety cooked countless times in the Canadian wild by tired and hungry trappers and traders. Back then, at least until stocks ran short, it would almost certainly have been accompanied by that equally ubiquitous backwoods staple, a fresh-cut slab of fried bacon.

**Ingredients:**
- 2 mugs of plain flour (we tend to stick to white, but you don't have to)
- 2 teaspoons or so of baking powder (you can leave this out if using self-raising flour)
- ½ teaspoon of salt
- About a mug of milky liquid (roughly half and half milk and water, or milk powder mixed in water)
- A healthy glug (perhaps ¼ mug) of vegetable oil

**Kit:**
- Frying pan

**To cook:**

If you use milk powder, perhaps a mug full, you can mix the dry ingredients before setting out, storing them in an airtight container and simply adding water at the campsite.

Either way, you could also add an egg if you like (reducing the liquid volume a little), but the basic version will do.

Mix everything you've chosen together to form a soft dough, adding a little more liquid if it feels a touch firm. If in doubt, err on the slightly gooey side. This can then be shaped into a disc that's slightly smaller than the frying pan.

To cook, pour a generous dollop of vegetable oil into your frying pan, heat it a little and slide in your bannock. Keeping everything away from a high heat (best over embers and avoiding flames) let it sizzle gently for a while. It should rise a touch, and you can turn it after a while (you'll have to guess, or peek under the edge) to let the other side brown too. To be sure that it's cooked through, a knife shoved into the centre, should come out clean, or at least only oily.

Then enjoy the results, while I await the emails, letters and phone calls telling me where I've gone wrong.

**Variations:**

Bannock can be kept simple, eaten savoury on its own or with your main meal, or you could add fruit and/or honey or sugar if you feel the need for something sweet. Sometimes we add a little cinnamon to the apple version, stewing the apples with some sugar first before adding them to the bannock mix. As with the stewed apple recipe, you could add pretty much any other wild or cultivated fruit you might fancy.

A sweet bannock, with apple.

*A Dutch oven oat loaf, fresh from the fire.*

*When your dough has risen for the second time.*

*Covering the lid with some good glowing embers – but not too many.*

### Dutch oven oat loaf

Ingredients:
- 1 mug strong white bread flour or wholemeal bread flour
- Half a mug of rolled oats
- Teaspoon dry yeast powder (perhaps Allinson's again)
- Teaspoon of salt
- Maybe as much as a mug of water
- A few drops of vegetable oil, or a smear of butter

Kit:
- Dutch oven
- ½lb bread tin
- Two six-inch nails (or something similar)

### To cook:

Start out in the same way as for the reflector oven loaf above, remembering this time to add the oats to your dough mix. As the oats tend to soak up a fair bit of water, and will take some time doing so, you will probably need to add as much as a mugful, possibly a touch more.

Carry on as before, while preheating your Dutch oven over a mature fire with plenty of hardwood embers.

When your dough has risen for the second time, place your tin in the oven, resting on the nails, or something similar, to keep it just off the bottom, then seal with the lid, covering the lid with some good glowing embers – but not too many.

Depending on the heat of your fire, it will take anything from about 15–45 minutes to cook your loaf, but best to check under that lid after about 10 minutes.

If you find that the loaf, once tipped out, is still a little undercooked on the sides and bottom, it can be popped back into the tin and placed carefully back on a cooler edge of the embers for a minute or two, perhaps piling some glowing bits against the side. Don't leave it too long like this though.

*Chapati*

Chapati are the standard bread accompaniment to food all over the Indian sub-continent, cooked over perhaps millions of open fires every night. Traditionally they are made from atta, a very fine purpose made whole-wheat chapati flour. If you have atta that's grand, but a fine wheatmeal flour will do, preferably sifted through a sieve if you carry one. Wheatmeal, sometimes called brown flour, is a fine mix of white flour and wheat bran. It's less coarse than wholemeal.

The other fun bit about chapati is that they are very quick to cook, and it takes place in two stages. Once the dough is ready, it's baked first in an open pan. In India, this will be a tava, a slightly concave iron pan, something like a heavy flattened wok. A heavy frying pan will do, with a cast-iron version acting as the best substitute. Once cooked briefly on each side, the chapati is then exposed to intense heat to puff it up. Until you are used to this, it can be a little hit and miss.

We were taught to cook chapati by a Bombay couple who once had a cook called Bimla. Her chapati always puffed up beautifully. As a result, at least in that one Bombay home, successfully expanded chapatti were said to have Bimlad. Even the process itself gained a new verb, and referring to the final stage we still Bimla all our chapati.

A plate of chapati, still warm from the fire.

Bimlaing.

### Ingredients:
- A good heaped mug of atta (if you have it) or sifted wheatmeal flour
- Maybe a third of a mug of water (you can always add a little)

### Kit:
- A bowl
- Some sort of rolling pin (perhaps a metal water bottle)
- As heavy a frying pan as you can find
- An oven shelf wire grill

What To Cook 149

Chapati cooking in an Indian tava, with pale spots showing, and almost ready to Bimla.

**To cook:**

Mix the flour and about half your water, adding more water until you have a soft dough mix. Depending on your flour, you may need more than a third of a mug. Knead this for a few minutes, then cover the bowl with a damp cloth and leave for about half an hour.

While you heat your pan over a hottish fire, knead the dough again and divide into about 8–10 equal parts. As the dough should be sticky, you will probably need to dust hands and working surface with a little more flour.

Once the pan is hot, move it to sit over a quiet part of the fire, and place the oven shelf grill over the hot embers, then take a dough chunk and mould it into ball, which you then flatten with your palm. Using whatever rolling pin you can devise, and with further flour dusting, roll this into a thin disc about 13–15cm (5–6 inches) in diameter.

Lift this disc carefully, and slap it on your heated pan, letting it cook for anything between 30–60 seconds. It's ready when dry white spots develop, which you will only test by turning it. I do this with my hands, carefully. It will take less time, about 15–30 seconds, to cook the other side. The spots may brown a little. The other sign that things are ready for the next stage is when little areas of the chapati start to puff up.

And now for the fun! Lift your part-cooked chapatti and drop it onto the grill. With luck, and within seconds, it should Bimla. Turn it for a brief cook on the other side, and it's done. Eat while warm.

Isn't it funny how cooking the simplest dishes often requires the most description.

### Stick-bread

This is the bread for the backpacker, easy to prepare, and simple to cook using nothing more than a length of ash, hazel or any other straight growing stick from the hedge. It tastes pretty good too. It's also one of the best recipes and cooking methods to employ when encouraging youngsters, or young-at-heart oldsters, to appreciate the joy of campfire cooking. The ingredients listed here will make about six twisty mini-loaves, but the actual number will depend on preference and dough twisting skills.

**Ingredients:**
- A mug of either plain or self-raising flour
- A teaspoon of baking powder (if using plain flour)
- About half a mug of water
- A good pinch of salt
- A dash of olive oil

**Kit:**
- A bowl
- A stick, about finger thick at the thin end, and a little longer than your arm

Left: stick bread cooking – fun for adults too.

Right: they don't taste bad either.

What To Cook 151

*The dough wrapped around a stick, and about to meet the fire.*

**To cook:**

Mix the flour in your bowl with about half your water and all the other ingredients, before adding more water until you have a good pliable but not too soft dough mix. Divide the dough into hand-grab sized lumps (smaller than a tennis ball) and work these into long sausages, tapering them at the ends. These can then be twisted around the end of your stick. A little water on the underside of the dough will help if the ends won't stick... to your stick. It's best if each revolution doesn't overlap, when the dough can sometimes become a little too thick to cook through properly, but it doesn't matter if they touch.

Now simply hold the bread over, but not too near, the usual good bed of embers, turning frequently. The key to success is patience, and cooking time should probably be not less than 15 minutes.

**Variations:**

Like bannock, this plain recipe is very much open to onsite adaption and experimentation. You could add pesto, cheese or chopped sun-dried tomatoes to this savoury base, or exchange the olive oil for butter, adding sugar or honey, and perhaps chopped fruit, nuts or chocolate to make a pudding. The options are almost endless.

## Little meals

### *Baked potatoes*

A campfire classic; and few dishes are easier to prepare or deliver such a good satisfaction to effort ratio. Baked potatoes can either accompany a large meal, or stand as a simple repast on their own (with lots of butter at least).

All that warm starchy enjoyment seems to stick in the mind as well as it sticks to the ribs. Even as I write, my thoughts are wandering to the banks of the Ounasjoki in Arctic Finland, picturing the glowing embers piled over those promising foil packages, the sun sinking towards the hills. A darkening sky, forest behind, a meandering current to the front, the steam rising from a freshly split baked potato as the butter melts into the interior.

Ingredients:
- Large potatoes

Kit:
- Tin foil

**To cook:**

Let a mature fire die down until you have a good deep bed of glowing embers.

Wrapped in foil, and ready for cooking.

Take your potatoes and give them a light clean if they need it. A slit or two cut on one side will help steam escape (a requirement according to Susannah, although I'm not entirely convinced it's necessary).

Wrap the potatoes individually in the foil, trying to ensure that all areas are covered by at least two layers. Put them in the embers and bury them.

Turning and rolling your foil packages in the embers every now and again will aid even cooking. Pull one out and check it after about twenty minutes. Depending on position and fire characteristics, it may take as long as an hour to cook to perfection.

If you can achieve a collection of properly cooked potatoes, without any burnt skin, you're doing well. But then what look to be badly charred skins can often taste great.

Hot from the fire.

**Eggs baked in tomatoes**

Another very easy campfire meal, or addition to a meal.

The photos here were taken close alongside the Piteälven in northern Sweden. Both tomatoes and eggs (and foil I think) came from the Co-op store in Arjeplog, one of our favourite places to stock up on provisions before setting out into the wild. While these northern tomatoes looked like... well... tomatoes, we were both whisked unexpectedly back to childhood when we opened the rough green cardboard container. These days, almost all eggs sold in Britain are brown, so it was a nostalgic surprise to find the bright white shells nestled inside.

**Ingredients:**
- Largish tomatoes
- Eggs
- Salt and pepper

**Kit:**
- Tin foil

**To cook:**

Lop the top off your tomatoes and use a spoon to scoop out the soft interior. This convenient vegetable (or fruit) pot can then be filled with a raw egg and little salt and pepper. All you then have to do is replace the lid and wrap your filled tomato with foil.

Place your small foil bundles in the embers, covering them slightly and leave for about fifteen to twenty minutes, rotating occasionally to help even cooking.

If you happen to find a jar of salted anchovies in your food box, one dropped into the hollow tomato before the egg is added will give a pleasant Mediterranean pep.

*Toast*

I know, hardly a culinary challenge, but then this is another wood-fire camp classic with an unmatched gratification to effort ratio. How many campers over the centuries must have started their campfire cooking experience by using the embers to put some colour to a slice of bread?

**Ingredients:**
- Bread

**Kit:**
- Either an oven shelf grill, or
- A yard or so length of thin straight branch, forked at the end, with forks cut to the right length and left sharp

**To cook:**

A mature fire with a bed of glowing embers is best.

Slice the bread.

Lay the bread slices on the oven shelf, ensuring that it is lifted quite a way clear of the embers to avoid burning. Turn frequently until the desired colour. This is all very easy, if the shelf isn't placed too close at least.

The forked stick is perhaps easier, as long as the slice of bread doesn't fall off. Unlike the oven shelf method, it is much easier to keep an eye on the brownness of your toast, turning the slice and pinning it back to cook the other side.

Best with good butter of course.

To make a forked stick, just split a thin sapling at one end, then push a short section of twig, sideways on, down between the divide the keep the two prongs apart (this twig can just be made out in the accompanying photo). The two ends can then be sharpened slightly.

Early morning toast.

Something toasty to go with breakfast.

What To Cook 155

A late night photo of our roasted tomatoes, feta and pine nuts.

### Roast tomatoes, feta and pine nuts

All the taste of the Mediterranean, near Mevagissey, Malaig or Mora.

### Ingredients:
- Cherry tomatoes
- A small pack of feta cheese
- A handful of pine nuts
- Olive oil
- Thyme
- Black pepper

### Kit:
- Some sort of pan, preferably with a heavy base
- Svante Fredén reflector oven
- Square cake tin – 20cm (8 inches) about 2.5cm (1 inch) deep

### To cook:

Chop your tomatoes in half and pack them into the cake tin, cut side up, dust with a sprinkle of thyme and cook slowly in the reflector oven alongside a low to medium fire. You may feel tempted to add olive oil now, but try to resist. It can go on later.

While the tomatoes are being roasted gently to within a whisker of destruction, cut up the feta into small cubes and toast the pine nuts dry in your pan till golden.

When your tomatoes are shrunken and almost burnt, dig them, and all the caramelised juice, out of the tin and mix with the cheese, pine nuts and a good glug of oil, and finish by seasoning liberally with ground black pepper.

What To Cook

*Roast potatoes*

For a long time I thought these glorious additions to a meal where really reserved for home cooking. I'd tried cooking them over a fire using other methods before, but never with complete success. That is until Peter Carol of ProAdventure helped reintroduce me to the reflector oven. Not only is a genuine roast potato now something that can be enjoyed anywhere from Alpine Switzerland to Arctic Sweden, but they can be really good roast potatoes too.

**Ingredients:**
- Almost any potatoes, but definitely best if they are the floury sort
- Vegetable oil
- Salt

**Kit:**
- Saucepan
- Svante Fredén reflector oven
- 20cm (8 inch) square cake tin, about 2.5cm (1 inch) deep

**To cook:**

Chop your potatoes into whatever shape or size you prefer for roasting, and boil in a pan for about five minutes, or until the sharper edges start to soften. During the short wait, pour a good quarter inch (0.5cm) of vegetable oil into the cake tin and warm in the reflector oven alongside.

Then drain the water, and with either a lid, or very carefully, shake the potatoes inside a couple of times, to help those edges crumble a touch (when they will then crisp up beautifully while roasting).

Tip your little beauties into the warm oil, season with a pinch or two of salt, and place them back in the oven next to a lively fire. Cook for about twenty minutes to half an hour, basting frequently, and moving the less-cooked potatoes to the front of the dish.

Roast potatoes, with spicy beans.

Potatoes roasting with some carrots.

What To Cook

### Dulce and potato burgers

I mentioned in the ingredients section that we'd describe a couple of dishes that include found food, and here's one. This has become a real seaside camp favourite, for which John Wright, the author of *Edible Seashore*, needs to be thanked.

Very few seaweeds are bad for you, and even fewer that grow away from the tropics. Besides, dulce (*Palmaria palmata*), with it's broad, flat, red fronds, should be pretty easy to identify. It can be found along much of the British coast and beyond, with nothing else looking much like it.

Now I'm aware that many people struggle to get very excited about seaweed, and while I enjoy many of them on a plate, I think I understand. Laver, that classic West Country and Welsh dish is an acquired taste for most for example, and takes so long to cook that we tend to refer to it as 'What a PaLaver'. For that reason alone, it's not the ideal campfire dish. Dulce on the other hand, is simplicity itself to cook, and really does taste good – the essence of sea.

Dulce and potato burgers.

**Ingredients:**
- One onion, sliced and chopped thin
- A couple of small to medium potatoes, chopped into small cubes
- A mug of dulce (packed in tight, this will be about the right amount), cut into small shreds
- Vegetable oil
- Black pepper

**Kit:**
- A small saucepan
- A frying pan

**To cook:**

Fry your onions until soft, while you simmer your dulce and potatoes until you can push a fork easily into the potato pieces.

Mash everything together roughly, adding a little ground pepper, leaving plenty of texture to the potatoes, then shape the mix into burgers about 8cm (3 inches) across and no more than 2.5cm (1 inch) thick.

Fry your burgers in the oil over a medium fire until the potatoes are golden and crispy.

Give me a call to come and help eat them.

Collecting dulce.

Slightly scruffy examples of kelp (on the right) and the more crinkly sugar kelp, collected from a Devon beach.

### Kelp crisps

Another one for the coastal forager, and as kelp seems to grow just about anywhere wet and salty, the main ingredient should be pretty easy to come by – although you may get wet in the process. Low tides and canoes make a good combination for the hunt, but fresh kelp can often be found washed up on the shore following a storm. The best kelp for crisping comes from the younger, smaller fronds.

Kelp comes in a variety of species in Western Europe, but *Laminaria digitata* is the most common around British shores, and is fine for this very simple dish. Sugar kelp, with the exotic dancer's name *Sacharina latissima*, produces the best crisps though, and you can use dulce very successfully too.

The cooking process is easy, but does use a lot of oil. It might also be classed as a dangerous sport.

**Ingredients:**
- Kelp
- Vegetable oil

**Kit:**
- A deep saucepan
- Any paired combination of wooden spoons or spatulas (and maybe a pair of leather gloves)

**To cook:**

Without washing them, air dry a small young frond or two for a short while, just to remove the surface moisture, then cut these into two 5–8cm (3 inch) squares.

Pour enough oil into your deep pan to produce a depth of at least 5cm (2 inches), and heat this over a moderate fire. Start with a single kelp test square, and if the surface blisters and bubbles almost immediately, the oil is hot enough.

Then, working with small batches of no more than three or four crisps at a time, drop these in, whipping them out again with your paired wooden implements, within

160   What To Cook

no more than six seconds. Any crisps left too long, and even slightly overcooked, should be rejected as they'll taste pretty grim and ruin this fine snack sensation.

Just so you know, the cooking process can spit a bit, especially if the surface of your seaweed is still a touch damp. Actually, it would be fairer to say that your crisps will spit... a lot. A pair of leather gloves (not man-made please, which could melt, or worse) may help. A welder's mask wouldn't go amiss.

Your crisps shouldn't need salting, as their upbringing ought to ensure they carry enough natural seasoning already. Then eat them soon. Left around for any time and your crisps will soon lose their pleasing crunch.

Last word, and it should almost go without saying, but with a cooking process that involves a pan of hot oil propped over a concentrated collection of flames, particular care needs to be taken to see the two don't meet.

A few kelp crisps, still warm from the pan.

What To Cook 161

***Chanterelle omelette***

With slight trepidation, but recalling the taste, I'm going to include a wild mushroom recipe. Besides, between midsummer and the New Year, many a fuel collecting foray into the woods will be met by the yellow glint from this particular fungi, pushing its way out from amongst the rotting leaf litter, and you don't really want to miss the opportunity.

Chanterelle (*Cantharellus cibarious*) are also pretty easy to identify with confidence. Care though needs to be taken to avoid the false chanterelle (*Hygrophoropsis auurantiaca*: mildly poisonous to some), which are more orange than yellow, and the jack o'lantern (*Omphalotus olearius*), another possible imposter, which is poisonous, but, helpfully, doesn't smell very pleasant. Once again, if in doubt, please cook something else.

Chanterelle (*Cantharellus cibarious*).

Chanterelle omelette.

**Ingredients:**
- A good handful or two of chanterelle, sliced thin
- Three or four eggs
- Butter
- Salt and pepper to taste

**Kit:**
- Frying pan

**To cook:**

Simplicity itself.

Fry the sliced chanterelle in the butter over a low fire. It helps if this process can be done gently, as these mushrooms can sometimes be a little tough until cooked through. Before they take any colour add the eggs, breaking the yolks and stirring slightly as they go in. Fold in the cooked edges, allowing the raw egg to run in and fill the gaps. We like our eggs only just cooked, but I'll leave that bit to you.

Serve with salt and ground black pepper.

### Nettle soup

Another classic foraged meal. This dish is best cooked in late spring and early summer, when the nettles are young. Full summer and autumn nettles are too stringy, and lose much of their fresh green flavour.

For the actual picking, unless very skilled, brave or foolhardy, wear gloves, and select only the tips and smaller fresh green leaves. Imagine you're a tea picker in Assam.

**Ingredients:**
- Two mugs of tightly pressed young nettle tips and leaves, shredded
- An onion, sliced thin
- One large floury potato, cubed small
- A knob of butter
- About three mugs (1½ pints, or a litre) of vegetable or chicken stock
- Salt and black pepper to taste, with chilli flakes as an option

**Kit:**
- A saucepan
- A good knife
- A wooden spoon

*A mug of fresh young nettle leaves (note the glove).*

**To cook:**

Before starting, find a good flat surface, the best being a wooden or plastic chopping board of some sort. Most indoor nettle soup recipes finish by blending the results. This is obviously impossible in camp, and although you can force the end results through a sieve if you have one, this is tedious and unnecessarily wasteful. We'll start instead by chopping our nettle haul as fine as possible. Like the picking, this can be carried out once endowed with the protection of gloves, or you can simply use the back of a wooden spatula to hold the bunches of leaves down tight, before going in with your knife. Just try to cut everything into tiny pieces.

What To Cook

Two bowls of nettle soup – good and warming on a wet day.

Once the cutting is done, fry the onion lightly in the butter until soft and slightly golden, adding the potato cubes and continuing until they have a little colour too.

Pour in the stock and pepper (and a pinch of chilli flakes if you wish) and, after bringing it all to the boil, simmer for about quarter of an hour, or until the potato cubes start to fall apart. I now mash the onions and particularly the potato as much as possible with the back of the wooden spoon, as this makes for a creamier soup, but you don't have to.

Add the nettles for only the last couple of minutes.

**Stuffed mushrooms**

Adaptability is the campers' asset here, assuming you have some mushrooms of course. This meal can be produced with standard cultivated mushrooms, chestnut mushrooms, both probably bought before setting out. The field mushroom (*Agericus campestris*) and horse mushroom (*Agaricus arvensis*) make fine foraged fungi stand in, although the horse mushrooms can produce quite a bit of liquid.

Then there's the filling, which can include any of the items listed below, lose one or two, and often benefit from the addition of basil, parsley, chopped chives or thyme if you have them. For this version we start with four Portobello mushrooms.

Stuffed mushrooms.

**Ingredients:**
- Four medium sized Portobello mushrooms
- Six or eight sun-dried tomatoes
- A handful of pine nuts
- A clove of garlic, chopped fine
- A tablespoon of tahini
- A good squeeze of lemon, if you have one
- Salt and pepper to taste

**Kit:**
- Svante Fredén reflector oven
- A 20cm (8 inch) square cake tin, about 2.5cm (one inch) deep

**To cook:**

Choose four mushrooms that squeeze into the tin, and sit them in ready to be cooked.

Chop the sun-dried tomatoes into small pieces and combine with the pine nuts, garlic, tahini, lime juice, and salt and pepper. There should be enough oil in the folds of the tomatoes, but if it all still feels a little dry, add some olive oil. Then spoon this mix into your mushrooms.

Stuffed mushrooms, feeling the heat.

Place the tin in the reflector oven, which should be next to your fire, and maintain a low to medium heat for twenty minutes to half an hour, or until the mushrooms soften and the filling bubbles and starts to take colour. You may need to turn the tin to cook everything evenly.

**Fish on a stick**

When I was a boy, just about every village lad and lass had 'perfected' this dish by the age of ten or eleven, cooking something of perhaps not quite take-able size, procured from the local river. Only the sea trout caught on bread paste, and with remarkable ease, by a very young brother, stand out particularly in the memory by bucking the usual small fry trend.

Crouched over a fire by a woodland den, close to the riverbank, hoping the smoke wouldn't attract the attention of the local keeper (we weren't too worried, we could run a lot faster than him) we'd imagine ourselves Mohicans, or, depending on allegiance, Swallows or Amazons, and transform our prize from its raw state to something approaching edibility.

With maturity (at least a little), and rather more cooking experience, this method of preparing a fish can be very successful. As can probably be imagined, such a simple technique, with easily acquired kit, makes this system ideal for the weight conscious traveller too. Mind you, as can also be recognised, this method is really only suited to the cooking of relatively small prey.

An Arctic grayling, cooked on a stick.

**Ingredients:**
- A smallish fish, gutted, and de-scaled if needed. Don't take the head off though.

**Kit:**
- A stick, not to thick, but not too thin either (down to experiment I'm afraid).

**To cook:**

Build a small fire, letting it die back to a good bed of embers.

With a sharp knife, split one end of your stick, taking the split back about 8–10cm (3–4 inches). Once happy with your split, sharpen those ends. Pass this pointed end through the mouth of your fish, along the body to the end of the abdominal cavity,

What To Cook

Now simply grill your fish.

and, perhaps with the aid of your knife, divide it, pushing each pointed half into the flesh beyond to either side of the spine. This should stop the fish rolling around your stick as it's turned.

Now simply grill your fish over the embers, using the distance from the glow to control the temperature. Try to take things fairly slow, rotating your fish to allow the flesh to cook right through, taking care to cook both the back and the interior of your meal fully.

We tend to continue in the spirit of the technique, eating the juicy flesh with our fingers (which also makes it easy to feel and avoid the inevitable bones).

# Big meals

These are the heftier main meals.

### *Aubergine, courgette and lentil curry*

Using vegetables with a high colour and flavour content, this curry has a number of other camp benefits that ensure its inclusion here. Employing easy to carry and cook lentils, the whole thing is surprisingly simple. The dish also allows Susannah's combined coconut oil and creamed bar to perform to its full potential. The initial idea for this dish came from the Hemsley sisters, who may, or may not, be keen campers.

To make things even more attractive to the camp cook, the whole thing can also be cooked in a single pot.

### Ingredients:

- A generous handful of cashews
- A bar of combined coconut oil and creamed coconut (the latter chopped roughly)
- Two large onions, sliced thin
- A large chunk of ginger, grated or cut very small
- A generous amount of garlic, crushed and chopped a little
- One to two hot chillies (or chilli powder to taste)
- A level mug of red lentils
- About two mugs (a pint, or 600ml) of chicken or vegetable stock
- A large aubergine, diced
- A couple of courgettes, diced and/or sliced
- A good handful of cherry tomatoes, left whole
- Lemon juice and tamari (or ordinary soy sauce) to season

### Kit:

- A large pot with a lid. We use a French casserole pot

### To cook:

Before cooking everything else, dry fry the cashews in your pot over a low heat. Then set these aside.

Cutting up chillies for an aubergine, courgette and lentil curry.

What To Cook  169

Aubergine, courgette and lentil curry, with the addition of a good handful or two of wilted spinach leaves.

Break off the coconut oil and fry your onions until lightly golden, adding the courgettes and aubergine to gain a little colour, and the chillies or chilli powder, garlic and ginger towards the end. Then tip in the lentils, followed by the stock and creamed coconut. Keep all this stirring, and add more water if things start to look a bit dry, at the same time trying not to let everything grow too sloppy.

After about ten minutes, throw in the whole cherry tomatoes, and cook for about another five minutes or so, or until the lentils are cooked, and the curry has a good gooey consistency.

Serve with the cooked cashews on top, and lemon juice and tamari if you have it.

## Leek risotto

This simple risotto is a great campfire dish. It's easy to cook, and the main ingredient, the rice, is easy to store. The leeks also last well if stored somewhere cool and dry.

All those finished risotto flavours also really start to sing with the addition of some grated Parmesan. This is one of the best cheeses to carry into the wild as it will last a lot longer than any softer cheese.

**Ingredients:**
- A couple of leeks
- Two cloves of garlic, crushed and chopped a bit
- A heaped mug of arborio rice (or other risotto rice)
- Olive oil (or butter if you have it)
- About three mugs (a pint and a half, or roughly a litre) of chicken stock (made using cubes or similar)
- Grated Parmesan, if you have it
- Salt and pepper to taste

**Kit:**
- Saucepan, casserole or deep frying pan over fire irons, but would cook well in a Dutch oven too
- A wooden spoon or spatula

*Leek risotto, with plenty of Parmesan cheese.*

**To cook:**

Clean and slice your leeks finely, then fry them in your oil or butter until they have softened and taken a touch of colour. Throw in the garlic, fry on for a minute or so, and then add the rice and stir it all well to coat each grain with the fat.

Now start to add your stock, pouring in a little at a time over a low heat, keeping everything moving about regularly, and adding a little more as things grow sticky. Once the stock has gone, try a grain or two of rice, and, if still crunchy, add a little more water until done.

Add the cheese and whatever seasoning you see fit

*Frying the leeks.*

What To Cook

*Adding a little seasoning to a chirozo risotto.*

### Chorizo risotto

While a simple leek risotto tastes excellent, and is probably Susannah's favourite, the other benefit of this meal is that it works so well with the addition of the sort of meat you can carry easily and successfully into the wild. Both smoked bacon and a dried sausage such as French saucisson work wonderfully with the leeks; all that fatty flavour also soaked up by the rice. My favourite addition is Spanish (or better still Basque) chorizo, especially the picante, or spicy, variety.

**Ingredients:**
- An onion, sliced thin
- About a third of a picante chorizo, cut into slightly chunky rounds
- A handful or two of field mushrooms, cut into chunks
- A couple of cloves of garlic, crushed and chopped
- A heaped mug of arborio rice (or other risotto rice)
- Olive oil (or even better, butter if you have it)
- About three mugs (a pint and a half, or roughly a litre) of chicken stock (made using cubes or similar)
- Grated Parmesan, if you have it
- Salt and pepper to taste

**Kit:**
- Saucepan, casserole or deep frying pan over fire irons, but would cook well in a Dutch oven too
- A wooden spoon or spatula

**To cook:**

Fry your sliced onion in your oil or butter until they have softened and taken a touch of colour. Then add the chorizo chunks and mushrooms, and continue to fry for a couple of minutes. Add the rice and continue to cook as for the leek version above.

Chorizo risotto.

**Variations:**

This fairly basic risotto dish can be adapted almost endlessly, depending on what you still have left in your wannigan or can find in the woods nearby. Almost any dried meat, or fresh meat for that matter, can be added, as could a number of vegetables. Other mushroom varieties, in numerous shapes and forms, are also ideal (some even from the wild if you know what you're doing), either as accompaniments or to provide the main flavour for the dish. For those that can spot cep, otherwise known as porcini or Karl Johan, these make a truly wonderful addition.

Cooking a leek end curry on an Arctic island beach.

Our Indian spice tin.

### Leek end curry

Another hearty meal in one pan and, for reasons that will become obvious, a great one to cook the night after you've eaten a leek risotto (assuming you haven't disposed of those slightly tough, dark green leek tops).

This meal is proposed in the expectation that, like us, you will have carried a pretty comprehensive selection of spices into the wild. Our stainless steel Indian spice tin, or masala dabba, designed for just this sort of task, features in the accompanying photos.

Ingredients:
- Two, or maybe even three, teaspoons of paprika
- A healthy teaspoon of ground turmeric
- A teaspoon or two of black mustard seeds
- A good pinch of cinnamon powder
- A generous grind of black pepper
- A couple of hot chillies, or chilli flakes/chilli powder to taste
- One onion, sliced thin
- A good glug of olive oil (or whatever vegetable oil you fancy)
- Two cloves of garlic, crushed and chopped
- The dark green tops from two or three leeks, shredded small
- One or two carrots, sliced into rounds
- About two mugs (maybe a bit less than a pint, or ½ litre) of chicken stock
- Half to one mug of pearl barley, depending how hungry you are
- Salt to taste

Kit:
- Casserole, heavy saucepan or Dutch oven

174   What To Cook

Leek end curry, ready to warm the cockles.

**To cook:**

Fry your onion in the oil till it takes a little colour, then add the leek ends and cook slowly until softened, again perhaps gaining a little colour. You can add the garlic towards the end of the process. Tip in the carrots, stirring once or twice, before adding the pearl barley and coating these with the oil.

Throw in all your spices and stir for a while, frying until well mixed, and then pour in your stock. Bring to the boil, then put on a lid and simmer until the carrots and barley are cooked, which may take up to half an hour. We prefer it all to be still a little chewy. We also like to remove the lid towards the end of the process in order to reduce the spicy liquid. The pearl barley helps produce a warm and wonderful, oily sauce, with a slightly grainy texture all of its own.

Spicy beans.

***Spicy beans***

We will occasionally make this wholesome and filling meal using a tin of cooked cannellini or haricot beans, but we are much more likely to bring them back to life, zombie like, from dry. This usually entails pouring a mugful of dried beans into a clip-lock plastic food container in the morning, adding a couple of mugs of water before sealing it up and storing it in our canoe for the day's journey. They are ready to cook when we arrive, hungry, at the next waterside campsite.

**Ingredients:**
- That mug of rehydrated beans (or a tin of precooked)
- A good glug of olive oil
- Black pepper
- Two large onions, sliced
- Half a dozen field mushrooms, sliced or chopped
- Two or three cloves of garlic, crushed and chopped
- A pinch of thyme or basil, dry or fresh
- A teaspoon of paprika, preferably smoked
- A good pinch of chilli flakes
- A teaspoon of ground cumin
- One mug (half a pint, or 300ml) or so of stock (whatever you fancy or have to hand)
- A good handful of chopped tomatoes
- A carton of passata (puréed tomato)
- Salt and pepper to taste

**Kit:**
- A deep pan of some sort

Spicy beans (with grilled perch).

**To cook:**

If you are using rehydrated beans, cook these as instructed on the packet, which usually means boiling them for half to three-quarters of an hour. Tinned beans are almost always precooked.

Fry your onions in the oil until they gain plenty of colour, then add your mushrooms and ground black pepper, and continue to fry until the mushrooms have shrunk down and browned a little. Finish the frying by stirring in the garlic for a minute or so.

Add the spices and stir for a bit, mixing them in well and frying a touch, before adding everything else but the beans, and simmering for half an hour. You could use a tin of chopped tomatoes instead of the whole tomatoes and passata.

Drop in your beans and cook for a final quarter to half an hour, reducing the sauce if needed, before adding salt to taste.

Reindeer burger ingredients.

***Reindeer burgers and lingonberry relish***

Although we don't often carry meat into the wild, there are exceptions. On visiting a small store in Arjeplog, it seemed only reasonable to buy some reindeer mince before heading north to find a new stretch of river. On a sandy beach that evening, we decided to turn this into burgers.

We had thought that we'd need an egg to help bind everything, but in the end, we just added some crushed Swedish mini crispbreads.

So what to go with them? Well, chips of course, fried gently in vegetable oil. These were great, but the star addition to this meal was a relish, designed on the spot, using the wonderfully tart, just ripe, lingonberries picked in the woods tight alongside.

### Ingredients:
*For the burgers:*
- A small pack of reindeer mince (other mince may be easier to find)
- A small onion, sliced thin
- One or two Swedish mini crispbreads
- Salt and pepper

*For the relish*
- A large onion
- Tablespoon of vinegar (malt will do, although we tend to carry something fancy)
- A tablespoon of sugar
- A mug of ripe lingonberries (*Vaccinium vitis-idaea*), also known as cowberry or partridgeberry The berries turn red when fully ripe, but don't worry if some are still a touch green

### Kit:
- A frying pan
- A small saucepan
- A wooden spoon or spatula

**To cook:**

When cooking burgers, we like to fry the sliced onions lightly first, but you can add this to your burger mix raw.

After crushing one or two mini dried breads, blend these into your mince and onion mix. With other minces you may need to add an egg to help everything to bind.

This blend can then be moulded by hand into balls, which are then flattened to produce a collection of burgers about finger to thumb thick. To cook, just fry gently in vegetable oil over a low to medium heat.

For the relish, chop your onion small and fry this gently in your small saucepan until they soften, then add your lingonberries and continue to cook, stirring frequently. Once everything is good and soft, simply add the vinegar and sugar and cook over a low heat until the whole mix has reduced and thickened.

Left: reindeer burgers and lingonberry relish, with chips.

Right: lingonberry relish starting to reduce.

The main ingredients for a blue cheese and mushroom quinotto, with a bowl of young spinach leaves to add right at the end of the cooking.

### Blue cheese and mushroom quinotto

Another great meal, and all the better for the camp because it is extremely simple, and can be cooked in one pan. This dish is essentially a risotto, only made with quinoa instead of rice, and hence the name. Another recipe adapted for outdoor life from a Hemsley original.

Ingredients:
- A generous knob of butter or glug of olive oil
- Two onions, chopped small
- Four cloves of garlic, crushed and chopped a little
- As many field mushrooms as you like, sliced
- A heaped mug of quinoa
- At least two mugs (a pint, or 600ml) of chicken or vegetable stock
- Tablespoon of vinegar
- A pinch of dried thyme
- A good handful of any blue cheese, crumbled into chunks
- Lemon juice, if you have it, and pepper to season (the cheese should ensure this dish is salty enough)

Kit:
- A large pot with a lid. We use a French casserole pot on fire irons, but could be cooked easily in a Dutch oven.

**To cook:**

Chop and fry the onions in whatever oil or fat you wish till they take a little colour. We tend to use butter or olive oil. Then add the mushrooms, and after a few more minutes the garlic (we leave the garlic till last in the belief that if over fried it can grow a little bitter).

180   What To Cook

Blue cheese and mushroom quinotto, cooked in our French cast iron casserole.

Add the quinoa, stirring to coat the grains in your oil or butter, before adding the vinegar first, then the water and thyme, and covering it all with a lid. Check every now and again to give a stir, adding a little more water if things grow too dry.

After about ten minutes the quinoa will start to release tiny spirals. At this point drop in your crumbled blue cheese, put the lid on for another minute or so, finishing by doing no more than folding in the molten lumps.

Along with the lentil curry on page 169, or the leek end curry on page 174, these one pot meals are ideally suited to the addition of green vegetables such as spinach or kale, right at the end of the cooking process. Young spinach can be stirred in to wilt for just the last couple of minutes. Older spinach, kale or chard, which will last longer in your camp food stores, will need to be removed from any tough stalks, shredded and added a little earlier.

What To Cook

*Ready to eat.*

***Grilled perch***

This simple meal has evolved over the years. The first change was that we began to cook perch at all. My experiences as a boy with English perch didn't endear me to these often muddy little predators. Trying the stunning, fresh, almost bass-like flavour of the firm white-fleshed fish in northern Scandinavia changed all that. Perch is now one of our favourite eating fish.

Following local Sámi (the indigenous people of Scandinavia) guidance, we started by baking these fish wrapped in tinfoil. Then, one day, we found we'd run out of this useful wrapping. Thinking this through, and taking a look at the rhino like skin of these fish, I decided to try grilling them as they were. Now we rarely cook perch any other way.

**Ingredients:**
- Perch

**Kit:**
- Oven shelf

**To cook:**

Gut and behead your fish. We usually remove the pectoral fins and bones too. As this is the first time we mention fish gutting in the big meals section, a short description of the method might not go amiss.

For any round fish, that is, anything but a flat fish like plaice, turn it belly side up, and insert the tip of a sharp knife into the vent towards the tail (there will only be one hole), the blade facing the head. Trying not to tear anything inside, cut through the skin to open a slot from vent to between the gills (see the accompanying photo). Then use your fingers to pull everything out, either ripping it away from the head end, or using your knife to cut the slippery mass free. You will usually now find that a fair bit of dark material (congealed blood) lies tight along either side of the spine. This is best removed (especially if you don't intend to eat your fish immediately) and can be achieved by dragging the sharp knife point along the spine to break the membrane. Water can then be used liberally to wash the blood away, and any other mess left in the overall gut cavity.

What To Cook

For a flat fish like sole or plaice, turn the fish belly (pale) side up and feel for a soft area behind the head. Cut a slice into this, and use a finger to hook out and pull away anything from the cavity.

But back to your perch.

Develop a good lively fire

Drop your perch on to the oven shelves (we prop ours on our fire irons). Then cook over a medium to high heat, turning often, and not forgetting to lay the fish open side down to cook from the inside too. Don't worry about the flames licking the perch's sides. Just let it grill until the skin is black and burnt. This can be peeled off easily, exposing what should be perfectly cooked, moist flakes of fish. We just add salt and pepper.

Left: starting the gutting process with a perch.

Right: grilling.

Mackerel and chips, cooked in Arctic Norway, with mustard in the batter.

***Battered coalfish***

Like all the fish recipes here, the coalfish has been used to stand in for just about anything finny and round from which you can take a fillet (we'll leave flatfish aside here, although please feel free to join in if you do know how to take a juicy slab of fish off a plaice or halibut).

To gain your fillet, take your coalfish, which should already be gutted, and cut across the body behind the head down to the spine. Then, with the top (dorsal) side of the fish towards you, take a long sharp knife and slice along the length of the fish as far as the spine (about half way across the body). You should now be able to use your fingers to pull/lift the fillet away from the fine rib bones on the other side of the spine, using the knife carefully to cut when the pulling runs the risk of tearing the flesh. With care, and a bit of luck, most of the fine bone will be left behind when you lift the fillet free.

Repeat on the other side of your fish, finishing by cutting away any fins and associated bones, feeling with your fingers to find and pull out any stray rib bones.

**Ingredients:**
- A mug of plain flour
- An egg
- About a mug of milk
- A good glug of vegetable oil
- Coalfish, or any other fish fillets
- When cooking an oily fish such as mackerel, I add a teaspoon of Dijon mustard to the batter, as this seems to balance the oily flavour of the fillet

**Kit:**
- Frying pan

What To Cook

Left: battered coalfish.

Right: wilderness filleting.

**To cook:**

Fillet your fish, or fish.

Mix your egg and flour together in the bowl, then add some of the milk, stirring it all in. Then add more until you have a mixture similar in consistency to double cream. Let this sit for a while and then add a little more milk if it's gone a touch stiff.

Add enough oil to your pan to cover the whole base generously and warm this over a moderate fire.

Dip your fillets into the batter mix, lifting it across to the pan once you're sure it's covered completely, and simply fry until golden.

What To Cook

A fish each.

Into the pan.

***Fried grayling***

Ingredients:
- Grayling, or just about any other fish
- Oil or butter

Kit:
- Frying pan

**To cook:**

Well this rather depends on the fish, but all will need to be gutted first.

Some fish, such as trout or mackerel can be dropped straight into the pan. Others, including grayling and perch, will need to be de-scaled first. If this isn't done, all the large tough scales will fall out during cooking and make the eating process more of a chore than a pleasure.

De-scaling can be quite tricky, mainly due to the slippery nature of a raw fish, but the aim is to scrape something like the back of a knife blade against the lie of the scales, or from tail to head, dislodging the scales as you go. The angle of the blade is critical, but once you get this right, the scales should just pop out in a great sparkly mass with each stroke. This sounds easy, and it is once you get the hang of it, but can often be quite frustrating as the fish can seem just as keen to get away as it was when alive. I often find that with the head taken off, the level cut across the 'shoulder' can be propped against something to help stop everything leaping away.

Once ready for the pan, add a little oil or butter to your cooking vessel and warm this over your fire, sliding your fish in to cook over a low to medium heat, turning frequently. Propped open, belly down, for a while, and spending some time on its back, should ensure that the deeper meat is cooked properly. A little inspection hole cut where the flesh is thickest near the spine will allow you to check that no pink or translucent bits are left.

### Grilled mackerel

**Ingredients:**
- Mackerel (one or two per person depending on size)

**Kit:**
- Oven shelf

**To cook:**

Gut and behead your fish. We usually remove the pectoral fins and bones too, but mackerel don't need de-scaling. The tails, left on the fish to be grabbed, can be very useful when turning the fish on the grill.

Develop a good bed of glowing embers. The fire can be pepped up as needed by additional stoking.

Drop your fish on to the oven shelves (we often prop ours on our fire irons). Then cook over a low to medium heat, keeping the fish turning to avoid the skin burning. The mackerel will twist, but turning them will help to minimise this. Try to make sure the fish spends at least some time on its back, and a good while with the open abdomen facing down, to ensure the flesh deepest in the fish cooks properly. Once done, we just add a little ground black pepper.

On a Devon beach, cooked over an oven shelf propped on stones.

Baking a fish in Arctic Norway, wrapped in foil, placed on a grill shelf propped on fire irons.

### *Baked bass*

**Ingredients:**
- Bass, or just about any round fish (sea or freshwater)
- Perhaps lemon or wild fennel, if you have or can find them

**Kit:**
- Tin foil
- Oven shelf

**To cook:**

Gut and de-scale your bass (no de-scaling needed for cod, pollock or many other sea fish, or for trout).

If you have a lemon you can place a chunk or two, including the skin, in the gut cavity. Where it can be found (often on costal cliff tops) wild fennel (*Foeniculum vulgare*) is great with fish, especially bass, and a sprig or two can also be added (but please be sure you can identify fennel with certainty).

Then, simply wrap your fish in the foil, perhaps with a double layer, and cook gently over a low fire for twenty to forty-five minutes, depending on the size of the fish. The only way to be certain your fish is cooked through fully is to open everything up to take a look.

Serve with salt and/or pepper to taste.

### Spicy chorizo mussels

Mixing fish and meat (surf and turf) has become quite fashionable, but as we don't carry much meat into the wild, this sort of trendy mélange isn't often seen in our camps. However, as we do pack away a chorizo quite often, it should be no surprise to see this Spanish (or Basque) speciality, particularly one of the spicy ones, making an appearance when we do try.

Because chilli seems to go well with shellfish, along with all that spicy oiliness from the pork fat, I've chosen mussels here to represent the surf part of the equation. You could do equally well with clams or cockles, or even limpets if feeling in need of a good chew.

In choosing your mussels, or any other shellfish, it's a sensible idea to take the old advice and avoid any month without an R in it. This should keep you safely away from the warmer months, when potential food poisoning risks are at their highest. Try also to find a good exposed beach, well away from river mouths, harbours or any other form of human settlement, preferably with a good tide rushing in and out regularly to keep the water clean. I'm not convinced that amateur purging (leaving the shellfish to clean themselves in salt water) is needed with shellfish from good clean areas, at least not if they are cooked alive, and cooked properly.

Spicy chorizo and mussels.

### Ingredients:

- An onion, sliced thin
- A good glug of olive oil
- Two cloves of garlic, crushed and chopped a bit
- A third to half of a picante chorizo, sliced chunkily
- A good hatful of mussels from a clean beach, scrubbed and de-bearded (I'll cover that below)
- Half a mug of water, or half water half white wine if you have it
- A double handful of tomatoes, chopped roughly, or perhaps a tin if you have one
- A good squeeze of lemon, if you have one

### Kit:

- A saucepan with a lid

What To Cook

Collecting mussels on the north Cornwall coast.

**To cook:**

The first task is to check and prepare your mussels. This isn't tricky. Throw away any gaping mussels, that is ones that don't close swiftly if tapped (otherwise known as dead). Give the outside of the shell a bit of a scrape to clean off anything loose, but don't worry about the odd barnacle or two. De-bearding is the removal of the hairy bits sticking out of the end of many of the mussels, used to attach them to the rock. These are extremely tough and well-attached inside, and I use a pair of pliers from my make and mend bag which always accompanies us when camping.

So back to the cooking.

Fry your onions in the oil over a medium fire until they have some colour. Then add the chorizo chunks and garlic and fry on for a couple of minutes.

Now add the water or wine/water mix and the chopped tomatoes and bring these to a boil. Drop in your mussels, cover with a tight lid, and cook for five minutes, adding the lemon juice at the end of the process.

When it comes time to serve, throw away any mussels that haven't opened. Well, you can't eat them anyway.

Good with fresh bread or rice.

### Thai tuna curry

This is the one fish dish here that doesn't use ingredients fresh from the nearest stream or bay. We don't carry many tins into the wild, they're just too heavy and bulky, but something containing tuna can save the day when nothing is biting and the idea of a fish supper has taken hold. Besides, not everyone enjoys sitting out there with a rod, or so I'm told.

Mind you, I can't really see where this fits in as a dedicated campfire recipe. Let's just say it's been cooked too often over one of our fires to be left out. And it is very quick and easy to prepare.

Thai tuna curry and rice, on a 17th-century Delft plate... copy... in melamine.

**Ingredients:**
- A couple of large onions, sliced thin
- A couple of handfuls of mushrooms, sliced thick
- A clove or two of garlic, crushed and chopped a little
- A tin of tuna (in brine, and line caught from a sustainable fishery please)
- A block of creamed coconut and oil
- A mug of water, perhaps a bit more
- A teaspoon or two of red Thai curry paste
- A mug of long grain rice

**Kit:**
- A small saucepan with a lid
- A frying pan

**To cook:**

One of the things that fascinate me about rice, is the wonderful variety of ways it can be cooked. Almost everyone will claim they have the 'best' or 'only' way to do it, most of which work equally well. This is our best and only way.

What To Cook

Take a mug of rice (we have a soft spot for proper basmati), and wash it carefully in the saucepan until all the surface starch has gone, and the milky water runs clear, or at least nearly clear. Then add about twice the amount of water to the pan and bring to the boil, immediately removing it to as low a heat as possible and leaving for ten to fifteen minutes, trying not to take off the lid too soon. A fork used to dig a little hole in the rice, will show whether the water has all be absorbed, when the rice should be perfect. You can always add a little more if the grains are still a little crunchy.

Alternatively, use your own 'best' or 'only' method, and cook your rice just how you like.

While the rice is approaching perfection, fry your onions in the coconut oil until lightly golden, adding the mushrooms for a while to shrink and gain colour, and then the garlic for a minute or so. Then add your curry paste, frying for perhaps another minute before adding the creamed coconut and water, and then tipping in the tuna. Heat the fish through fully and serve with your light fluffy rice.

Of course there is no reason why you couldn't use any fresh fish in this dish, filleting your catch first and cutting the results into chunks.

Frying onions for a tuna curry while the rice cooks slowly in a pot alongside. The basil plant travelled with us from Devon to Alta, growing ever smaller as we moved north (although it did at least survive unmolested on this evening).

## Puddings

### *Pancakes*

Surely one of the true camp cooking classics. There are many basic recipes out there, but we like to leave any sweet stuff from the initial mix, only adding something like maple syrup afterwards.

It's interesting that although this is essentially a very simple dish, describing the actual cooking turns out to be quite tricky. So much depends on a feel for the results, including the batter mix consistency, the amount of oil, oil heat, cooking time... I think you probably get the picture.

Don't be put off though, even poorly cooked pancakes usually taste great. Oh, and the first one is almost always a minor disaster.

**Ingredients:**
- A mug of plain flour
- An egg
- About a mug of milk
- Vegetable oil

**Kit:**
- Bowl
- Frying pan
- Wooden spatula

Surely one of the true camp cooking classics.

**To cook:**

Mix your egg and flour together in the bowl, then add some of the milk, stirring it all in. Add more milk until you have a mixture similar in consistency to double cream. Let this sit for a while and then pour in a little more milk if it's grown a touch stiff.

Turning to your frying pan, set this over a moderate heat and pour in enough oil to produce a thin film over the entire base. After letting this heat to the point where it's just beginning to smoke, give your mixture another stir, and then pour in a dollop. The amount is down to practice, and needs to spread to produce a thin even covering over much of the pan's cooking area.

Folded to enclose a handful of wild Arctic blueberries.

If your pan has a pretty good non-stick surface, the pancake should start to move as it cooks. Often, a good sharp shake of the pan will do the trick.

A little check under one edge will tell you if your pancake's done, and when you need to turn it. I'll leave this bit to you, but I'd probably avoid the traditional tossing method unless you're either used to it, or enjoy a good pinch of risk in your life. Repeat with the other side, and you're done.

I often add a touch more oil between individual pancakes, letting the fresh supply heat through for a moment or two before adding the next batter dollop.

If you're fortunate enough to have wild berries to hand, particularly blueberries, sprinkle these over the pancake just as the first side is starting to cook, when they embed themselves in the uncooked mixture. We then fold them over and keep turning this parcel till we guess the interior is cooked. Cloudberries work well when added like this too.

Serve as they are, or with a drizzle of real maple syrup. For this very moment, we were once given homemade maple sugar by a pair of generous Canadians. Wow, what a flavour!

### Blueberry (in oranges) muffins

This recipe allows for some pudding baking without the need for cumbersome pots or ovens. A little forethought is needed though, as you are required to not only collect six oranges, but to have eaten these by cutting them in half, scooping the interior out with a spoon, and keeping the two empty orange skin sections from each of your donor fruit.

Ingredients:
- Mug of plain flour
- 1½ teaspoons of baking powder
- ¼ mug of sugar
- One egg
- ¼ mug vegetable oil
- ¼ mug milk (fresh, or reconstituted milk powder)
- Blueberries (often *Vaccinium myrtillus*); also known in Britain as the bilberry, whortleberry or whinberry, and in Scotland the blaeberry. Not to be confused with the big, but boring, American blueberry (*Vaccinium corymbosum*) found in supermarkets... and America (but not Canada, which has *myrtilloides*). And if you think that's a lot of different blueberry varieties, this is just touching the surface. In Western Europe alone there are at least another half dozen common, or pretty common, blueberry types – all edible.

Kit:
- Bowl
- Whisk (or fork)
- Foil
- Six oranges skins, the insides already eaten

Blueberry muffins, still in their orange skins.

Or with wild raspberries.

**To cook:**

Whisk up everything but the blueberries and milk, adding the milk slowly to the mix until it is thick, but just pourable (you need to be patient, and give it a hand).

Ease the mix into six of the orange skin halves. Once filled, push about four or five blueberries into the top and then seal with the other skin as a lid.

Trying not to squash them, wrap each orange individually in foil, burying these in the embers for about fifteen to twenty minutes. You can pull out one after fifteen minutes to see if they're cooked.

### Blueberry and marzipan (in melon) sponge

Having cooked the orange skin muffins, involving all that earlier, and very careful, orange consumption, we didn't think much of the results. Not that the cooked muffins weren't delicious, they were – they were just very small, and didn't really seem to merit the effort.

Then, one day, having cut a very good melon in half, working through one side each with a spoon, Susannah took a look at the empty skins. This is the result.

**Ingredients:**
- Mug of plain flour
- 1½ teaspoons of baking powder
- ⅓ mug of sugar
- One egg
- ¼ mug vegetable oil
- ¼ mug milk (fresh, or reconstituted milk powder)
- Blueberries
- Generous block of marzipan, cut into small cubes

**Kit:**
- Bowl
- Whisk (or fork)
- Foil
- The skin of a melon, cut in half

**To cook:**

Whisk everything as you would with the muffins above, and then pour/tip the soft mix into one half of the melon. A good handful of blueberries and the marzipan cubes are then placed on top, with any cloudberries (*Rubus chamaemorus*) if you can find them.

With the other melon skin half set back on top as a lid, the whole thing is then wrapped in foil and buried in the embers, where it is left for half an hour to forty-five minutes.

Great with custard.

*A queen of wild campfire puddings*

*Adding the blueberries.*

*Fresh from the fire.*

What To Cook 197

Cooking in the reflector oven.

### Apple, blueberry and coconut bake

This satisfying camp pudding started life in Madeleine Shaw's book *Ready, Steady, Glow*, and has been adapted by Susannah for outdoor life. The recipe uses one of those camping friendly plastic wrapped coconut oil and cream combinations we like so much.

The pudding is cooked here in Svante Fredén's reflector oven, where an eye can be kept on everything while it bakes, but it could be prepared well enough inside a Dutch oven.

Ingredients:
- A mug and a half of rolled oats
- One 200g combined block of coconut oil and cream
- Half a mug of hot water
- One teaspoon baking powder
- A thumb-sized lump of ginger, grated
- One teaspoon ground cinnamon
- Two apples, grated or sliced thin and chopped
- A handful of blueberries
- Two eggs
- Nine teaspoons of honey
- A good handful of chopped walnuts or pecans
- A handful of pumpkin seeds
- A handful of coconut flakes
- Two pinches of salt

Kit:
- Svante Fredén reflector oven
- 20cm (8 inch) square cake tin, about 2.5cm (1 inch) deep
- Kettle
- Small pan
- A square of baking parchment (if you have it)
- Bowl

### To cook:

Start by heating your water and separating the coconut oil from the coconut cream. Then chop or grate the cream into the water, stirring and melting it to produce a coconut milk. You may need to add a little more hot water, aiming to end up with about three-quarters of a mugful.

Still hot.

The bake then proceeds in two halves.

In some sort of mixing bowl, combine the oats, baking powder, grated ginger, cinnamon, apples, blueberries, eggs, coconut milk, six teaspoons of honey and a pinch of salt. Stir well and pour this mix into your baking tray (lined with baking parchment, unless the tray is very non-stick).

In a pan, over a low fire, melt about half the coconut oil, and add the remaining three teaspoons of honey, the coconut flakes, seeds, nuts and a pinch of salt. Then pour this over the oat layer.

Cook this in the reflector oven alongside a low to medium flame, turning occasionally. It should take about half to three-quarters of an hour to bake through, the topping turning a golden brown. This bake is just as good with many other foraged berries, such as blackberries or wild currants.

### Stewed apple and blackberry

Admittedly, there's nothing particularly campfirey about this simple pudding, but it does draw on a common wild ingredient. Blackberries (*Rubus fruticosus*) are widely available to the hedgerow gleaner from August to October, and seem to have evolved especially to add colour and flavour to apple puddings.

This easy recipe doesn't need to be restricted to just these two fruits either. The apples could be replaced by pears for example, or plums, or peaches, the blackberries substituted with wild blackcurrant (*Ribes nigrum*), redcurrants (*Ribes rubrum*), blueberries, raspberries (*Rubus idaeus*) or even perhaps some escaped gooseberries (*Ribes uva-crispa*). The options are almost endless. Perhaps just throw them all in.

If you think all this is all sounding a little cavalier, there are no excuses, and the recipe will continue in much the same vein. Amounts of fruit, the ratios, even the

Stewed apple and blackberry.

cooking times can be adjusted enormously depending on availability, ripeness and taste. Just try not to burn it – and not because it might not still taste great, dragged from the bottom of the pan, but it can be very tedious cleaning that pot.

Ingredients:
- A few apples, skinned and sliced
- A handful or two of ripe blackberries
- A mug or so of water
- A tablespoon or so of sugar or honey

Kit:
- A saucepan
- A wooden spoon

*The options are almost endless. These are plums.*

**To cook:**

Place everything in a saucepan, and cook over a low fire, stirring frequently. As the water starts to disappear, stir continuously, and check the softness of your apples, adding a splash or two of water until they are done. Aim for a syrupy sauce, trying to avoid everything growing too hot and dry, or you may find you've produced some sort of fruit toffee.

Of course, if you wanted to dig out your reflector oven, and knock up a crumble topping, you could easily develop this dish.

### Baked apples

We used to cook these when I was as a boy, usually making quite a mess. Like so many campfire classics, which use the heat of the embers so effectively, the results are quite out of proportion to the relative lack of effort involved. Apple and sugar make excellent ember-bed fellows, and the healthy whiff of wood smoke flavours that make their way in through the foil seal only add to the overall experience.

**Ingredients:**
- One large apple per camper
- Sugar or maple syrup

**Kit:**
- Tin foil
- A good thin knife

**To cook:**

Take each apple, and, slicing in a circle around the stalk, cut deep down to remove a carrot-like plug containing the pips and much of the core. Try to ensure that you

An apple, stuffed with marzipan and wild blueberries, and baked in a Le Creuset casserole.

don't cut right through to the other side. The handle end of a teaspoon may help to excavate further, but try not to damage the edge at the top (you'll see why soon).

Pour your sugar or maple syrup into the excavated void until you've nearly reached the top. Then cut off the top quarter to about 1cm (half an inch) of your removed plug, perhaps even retaining the stalk, and use this as a plug to reseal everything.

Now wrap your apple in a good double layer of foil, and bury in the embers of your fire for about twenty minutes to half an hour. Be very careful in unwrapping these fruit bombs though, as the mix of molten sugar and cooked apple inside the skin can be quite explosive.

Still hot from the fire.

Alternatively, the apples can be baked inside a casserole or Dutch oven. We've used marzipan inside the apple instead of sugar when doing this too.

Serve with custard, or cream if you have it, or both.

After the meal.

# Bibliography

Only a small number of books have been mentioned, but they still deserve listing. I also want to recognise the cookery writers who have inspired meals directly, but receive only fleeting acknowledgement in the text. Very few recipes are unique, and many such as pancake and bannock mixes, loaf varieties, even risotto cooking methods, are pretty much ubiquitous. A few described here however, while they have been adapted to varying extents by Susannah and me for an outdoor existence, started life in the minds of other cooks. Their books are listed here.

*Camping and Woodcraft: A Handbook for Vacation, Campers and Travelers in the Wilderness,* Horace Kephart, Skyhorse Publishing 2017 (first published in full by Outing Publishing Company in 1917), ISBN 9781510722606

*Canoe Camping,* Tim Gent, Pesda Press 2014, ISBN 9781906095482

*Edible Seashore,* John Wright, Bloomsbury 2009, ISBN 9780747595311

*Ready, Steady, Glow,* Madeleine Shaw, Orion Books 2016, ISBN 9781409163381

*The Art of Eating Well,* Jasmine and Melissa Hemsley, Ebury Press 2014, ISBN 9780091958329

*The Singing Wilderness,* Sigurd Olson, University of Minnesota Press 1997 (first published in 1956 by Alfred A. Knopf), ISBN 9780816629923

Although not cited in the text, Richard Mabey's 1972 book *Food For Free* (Collins) deserves mention as a very useful place to obtain initial information on the subject of wild food. In addition to *Edible Seashore,* anything written about foraging by John Wright will be well worth seeking out.

# Index

## A
angle iron 35
apples, baked 202
apples, recipes 198, 200, 202
*Art of Eating Well, The* 205
ash 93
aubergine 169
axe 23, 27, 28
   felling 27
   Gränsfors Bruks 27
   handle 27
   head 27
   manufacturers 28
   sheath 28
   splitting with 68, 69, 70, 71, 72

## B
backpacker 20
bacon, smoked 172
bags, dry 46
Bahco, saw 26
baked potatoes, recipe 153
baking 119, 121, 122, 198
baking paper 45
bannock, recipe 146
bass, baked 188
beak-nosed hanger, support 112, 113
beans 129
beans, spicy 176
Ben Orford, knives 30
berries, recipes 195, 197, 200
berries, wild 134
bicycle 20
billy cans 41
blackberries, recipes 200
blowpipe, telescopic 22, 91
blueberries, recipes 195, 197, 198
board, cutting 39
boats 19
Bob Dustrude 26
bottles 133
bowl, mixing 45
bow saw 25
bow saw, use 67
Brades, axes 28
bread 132
bread, recipes 144, 148, 151
burgers, recipe 178
burns 86, 87
butter 128

## C
Caastrom, knives 30
camp crane, support 108
*Camping and Woodcraft* 35, 205
canoe 18
*Canoe Camping* 146, 205
cantilever, support 108
carrying capacity 16
cars 17
cast iron pots 44, 52
chapati, recipe 149
charcoal 93
chorizo 131, 172, 189
cleaning pots and pans 125
coalfish, battered 184
coconut, creamed 128
containers, food 46
containers, kit 46
cooking
   over fire irons 116
   under pot supports 118
   using a wood fire 101, 102
   what to 141
cooking ranges 52
courgette 169
crane, cooking under 118
curry paste 134
curry, recipes 169, 174, 191
cutting board 39
cutting tools 23

## D
dehydrated meals 54, 138
dehydrator 54, 138
detergent 124
dinghies 19
dry bags 46
dulce (seaweed) 158
Dutch oven 47, 51, 121, 122

## E
*Edible Seashore* 158, 205
eggs 131, 132, 154
eggs, powdered 132
Elwell, axes 28
embers 102, 116, 117, 119, 120, 122
Excalibur, dehydrators 54

## F
fats, cooking 128
feather stick 89
fire
   cooking with 101, 102
   finishing with 93
   lighting 21, 22, 87, 88, 89, 90, 91, 92
   problem solving 95
   where to light 79, 80, 81, 82
fire bowls 33, 34, 52, 123
fire irons 35, 36, 104, 105, 106, 116
fire irons, cooking over 116, 117
fire kit 21
fire-steel 22
firewood 61, 62, 63, 64, 66
first aid 84, 85, 86, 87
first aid kit 23
fish 130
fish, recipes 167, 182, 184, 186, 187, 188
flour 129
folding saws 26
folding trivet 37
food 127
   box 47, 136
   containers 47, 136
   dehydrated 54, 138
   foraging 134
   how much 137
   storage 136
*Food For Free* 205
foraging 134
fruit 130
frying pan 40
fuel, wood 61, 62, 63, 64, 65

## G
garlic 130
Gilpin, axes 28
Gränsfors Bruks, axes 27, 28
grater 45
grayling, fried 186
green log supports 115
griddle bowls 52
griddle pans 33, 34, 124
grill 36
grilling 106, 119

## H
handle, axe 27
hatchet 27
head, axe 27
head torch 45
Hemsley, Jasmine and Melissa 169, 180, 205
horizontal pole, support 110
Hultafors, axes 28
Husqvarna, axes 27, 28

## I

ingredients 127
iron, angle 35
irons, fire 35, 36, 104, 105, 106, 116

## J

jars 133
jug, measuring 45

## K

kale 181
kayak 19
Kelly Kettle 42
kelp, recipe 160
Kephart, Horace 35, 36, 205
kettles 41, 42
kindling 74, 89, 90
kit 13
kit, basic cooking 35
kit, containers 46
kit, fire 21
kit, first aid 23
kit list 55
   backpacker/cyclist 56
   kayaker 57
   vehicle supported camper 58
knife 29
   blade 30
   bushcraft 29
   cooking 38
   kitchen 30
   manufacturers 30
   paring 29, 38
   splitting with 72, 73
   Swiss-army 39
   type 29
   woodsman's 29

## L

Le Creuset, pot 52
leeks 171, 174
lentils 129, 169
lighter, gas 22, 90
lighting, fire 21, 22, 87, 88, 89, 90, 91, 92
Light My Fire 22
lingonberry relish 178
logs 66, 68, 69, 71, 72, 73
loppers 31

## M

Mabey, Richard 205
mackerel, grilled 187
matches 21, 90
measurements 142
meat 130, 131
Mora, knives 30
motorbike 20
MSR, pots 43
muffins, recipe 195
mushrooms, recipes 162, 165, 180
mushrooms, wild 134
mussels, cooking 189
mussels, foraging 190
Muurikka (griddle pans) 33, 34, 52, 123, 124

## N

nettle soup 163
nuts 133

## O

oats 129
oil, cooking 128
Olson, Sigurd 99, 205
omelette 162

onion 130
Opinel, knives 38
oven, Dutch 47, 51, 121, 122
oven, reflector 47, 48, 49, 50, 119, 120
oven shelves 36, 105, 106

## P

pancakes, recipe 193
pan, frying 40
pans 43
paper, baking 45
pasta 129
pearl barley 174
perch, grilled 182
Petromax, Dutch oven 51
Petromax, griddle pans 34
pole, cooking under 118
pole support, horizontal 110
pole support, single 111
portable stoves 32
potatoes, baked 153
potatoes, roast 157
pots 43
pots, cast iron 44, 52
pots, cleaning 125
pot supports 35, 103, 104, 105, 106, 107, 108, 109, 110, 111, 112, 113, 114, 115
Primus, kettle 42
problem solving, fire 95
pruners 31
pruning saw 26
pruning saw, use 68
pudding, baked 198
pudding, recipes 193
Puukko, knives 30

## Q

quinoa, recipe 180

## R

ranges, cooking 52
*Ready, Steady, Glow* 198, 205
recipes 143
reflector oven 47, 48, 49, 50, 119, 120
rice 129
rice, cooking 191
risotto, recipes 171, 172
roasting 121
roast potatoes, recipe 157
rucksack 20

## S

Sabatier, knife 29, 38
safety 83, 84
sailing 19
saucepans 43
saucisson, French 131, 172
saws 23, 25
   bow 25
   folding 26
   pruning 26
   use 67
seaweed 134, 158
secateurs 31
seeds 133
Shaw, Madeleine 198, 205
sheath, axe 28
shellfish 134
shelves, oven 36, 105, 106
Silky saw 26
*Singing Wilderness, The* 205
single pole crane, support 111
soap 125
soup, nettle 163
spatulas 44
Spear and Jackson, axes 28
spices 132
spinach 181
splitting wood 68, 69, 70, 71, 72, 73

sponge, recipe  197
spoons  44
stick-bread, recipe  151
stick, support  114
Stihl, saw  26
stock, cooking  133
stoves, portable  32
supports, pot  35, 103, 104, 105, 106, 107, 108, 109, 110, 111, 112, 113, 114, 115
Svante Fredén, ovens  50
Swiss-army knife  39

# T

tinder  76, 77, 88
tinder box (bag)  23
tin foil  44
titanium, pans  43

toast  155
tomatoes, recipes  154, 156
tomatoes, sun dried  134
tools, cutting  23
torch, head  45
transport  15
tripod, cooking under  118
tripod, support  107, 108
trivet  106, 107
trivet, folding  37
trucks  17
tuna, tinned  191

# V

vans  17
vegetables  129
vinegar  134

# W

wannigan (food box)  47, 136
washing up  124
wet ground  95
Wetterlings, axes  28
wet wood  95, 96
wind, fire  82, 83
wood
 fuel  61, 62, 63, 64, 65
 preparing  66
 rotten  64
 sourcing  63
 splitting  68, 69, 70, 71, 72, 73
 wet  95, 96
Wood Jewel, knives  30
Wright, John  158, 205

# Z

Zebra, billy cans  41